Basic
FLY FISHING

All the Skills and Gear You Need to Get Started

Jon Rounds

Lefty Kreh, consultant

Photographs by
Barry and Cathy Beck
and Jay Nichols

Illustrations by Dave Hall

STACKPOLE
BOOKS

Published by
STACKPOLE BOOKS
5067 Ritter Road
Mechanicsburg, PA 17055
www.stackpolebooks.com

Printed in China

First edition

10 9 8 7 6 5 4 3 2 1

Main cover photograph by Jay Nichols
Cover design by Tracy Patterson
Photographs by Barry and Cathy Beck, Jay Nichols, Ed Jaworowski,
   St. Croix Rod, Umpqua Feather Merchants
Illustrations by Dave Hall, Cliff Hauptman

Library of Congress Cataloging-in-Publication Data

Basic fly fishing : all the skills and gear you need to get
started / Lefty Kreh, consultant ; Jon Rounds, editor ;
photographs by Barry and Cathy Beck and Jay Nichols ;
illustrations by Dave Hall.— 1st ed.
     p. cm.
   ISBN-13: 978-0-8117-3303-8 (spiral-bound pbk.)
   ISBN-10: 0-8117-3303-3 (spiral-bound pbk.)
 1. Fly fishing. I. Kreh, Lefty. II. Rounds, Jon.

SH456.B2964 2006
799.12'4—dc22

2006001895

Contents

Acknowledgments

In my years as an editor at Stackpole Books, I had the good fortune to work with some of the best and most knowledgeable fly-fishing writers in the country, including Dave Hughes, Barry and Cathy Beck, Boyd Pfeiffer, Ed Jaworowski, Dick Talleur, Rich Osthoff, Ed Koch, Don Holbrook, and Norm Shires. One way or another, their work informs every page of this book, and I am in their debt. Many of their own books appear in the Resources section.

Likewise, the people at Stackpole Books again demonstrated why they have set the standard for fly-fishing books. Special thanks to Editorial Director Judith Schnell, Editor Chris Chappell, Assistant Editor Amy Lerner, Creative Services Director Tracy Patterson, and Senior Art Director Caroline Stover.

Lefty Kreh was generous with his time and bottomless knowledge of casting, and I was particularly fortunate to have Jay Nichols, Lefty's friend and the managing editor of *Fly Fisherman* magazine, shoot the casting photos. Likewise, thanks to Barry and Cathy Beck for providing the exquisite fishing shots that have become their trademark. Veteran fly-fishing illustrator Dave Hall was, as always, a pleasure to work with. I also thank Umpqua Fly Merchants for providing images of flies from their extensive catalog and Jeff Schluter of St. Croix for images of rods.

Finally, thanks to my lifelong friend and fly-fishing mentor, Bob King, for his timely and thorough responses to my many questions about trout-fishing techniques and fly patterns.

—Jon Rounds

Introduction

Watching a fly caster in action, you are struck by the grace of the line unfurling and the fly falling to the surface of the stream, but it looks difficult. Walking through a well-stocked fly shop, you are bewildered by the number of flies on display. Does each pattern imitate a different insect? How do you tell which ones the fish are feeding on? Who could know all this? In fact, many fishermen are so daunted by fly fishing they never attempt it. It just seems too much to learn.

The truth is, fly fishing is indeed one of the most absorbing outdoor sports in the world. More has been written about it than any other form of fishing, and you can go on learning about fly fishing for the rest of your life, investigating the subtleties of casting, presenting the fly, and the fine points of entomology.

Don't be intimidated. Getting started does involve an interlocking set of skills and knowledge about gear, knot tying, casting, fly selection, water reading, and tactics. But the idea behind this book is that out of that vast body of knowledge and skills, only certain ones are essential to launch yourself—to be able to pick up a fly rod, go to a stream, and catch some fish.

The first thing you need is a clear guide to essential gear and how to decide which outfit is right for you. Then you need to know how to tie a few knots and rig your outfit. After that, you can begin casting, which is the most difficult skill, but one that is eminently learnable, especially at the side of Lefty Kreh. After reading the first three chapters of this book, you should be ready to start fishing.

The last three chapters of the book are about fishing, with the focus on trout, the original and still the most popular type of fly fishing. Chapter 4 presents a practical overview of aquatic insects and trout-fly types, along with a guide to time-tested patterns in each category: dry flies, wet flies, nymphs, streamers, and terrestrials. Chapter 5 gives the beginner a coherent approach to finding and stalking trout, along with specific strategies for using all the fly types discussed in Chapter 4. Chapter 6 is an introduction to flies and tactics for bass and pike.

The goal of this book is not to oversimplify or dumb down a complex sport, but rather to distill the essential facts and skills from the vast amount available and get you out on the water as a competent fly fisher.

1

Gear

Flipping through a fly-fishing catalog, you could get the impression that this is a sport for the rich. A rod can cost $500, a reel $250, fly line $60. And then there are the breathable waders, aluminum fly boxes, Gore-Tex vests, not to mention leaders and flies. And if you delight in finely made tools and gadgets, on your first trip to a fly shop you'll think you've died and gone to heaven.

But if you want to learn fly fishing on a budget, relax. Only two pieces of fly-fishing equipment are necessarily costly: the rod and the line. And the rod can last a lifetime, the line several years. All the rest is a matter of comfort, status, and fun.

OUTFIT WEIGHT

Gear

Making sense of fly-fishing gear begins with an understanding of outfit weights. Very generally, the size of the outfit (rod, reel, and line) reflects the sizes of the flies, the fish, and the water. The lightest outfits are for casting tiny flies for small fish on small trout streams, whereas the heaviest outfits are for making long casts with big flies for big fish on big water.

You'll notice that fly-fishing outfits come in numbered sizes, 1 through 15, rather than in the more general designations of light, medium, and heavy, as in spinning and casting gear. This more precise system is necessary in fly fishing because, in order for an outfit to cast a fly effectively, the weight of the fly line must be closely matched to the weight of the rod. If the line is too light, the rod won't flex enough to generate power. Conversely, if the line is too heavy, the rod will flex too much, and you will lose control of the cast. Reels also come in numbered weights, and though matching the reel and rod is not as crucial to casting as matching the rod and line, the right weight reel will make the outfit feel balanced.

Above: Short rods are handy on small streams where long casts aren't required and tight quarters make long rods unwieldy.

Right: Surf fishermen need long rods to make long casts with big flies, often in windy conditions, as in this scene from the coast of Argentina.

Weights 4 through 8 are those most commonly used for freshwater fishing, whereas weights 9 through 12 are primarily for saltwater or large freshwater gamefish such as pike and muskie. Weights 1 through 3 are ultralight outfits, and weights above 12 are not really for casting but for trolling flies for large saltwater fish.

What Outfit Weight Should You Buy First?

When buying your first complete outfit, choose the weight best suited to your home water and the style of fishing you'll be doing most. Avoid trying to find an all-around outfit, one that will be good for several types of fishing; there is no such thing. Having the optimal equipment for the situation is especially important for beginners, as it will help you learn to cast and handle the fly more quickly and start catching fish. The whole experience will be more satisfying and less frustrating. You can always add new outfits as needs arise.

So first consider which stream, lake, or coastline you'll be fishing the most, and then find out which weight most fly fishers use there. Your local fly shop and the regional chapter of a fly-fishing association are good places to ask these questions.

Outfit Weights and Uses

Weight	Use
1, 2, 3	Ultralight trout; #18–28 flies; small, windless streams
4	Light trout; #12–20 flies; small and medium-size streams
5, 6	Medium trout; #6–18 flies; medium-size streams
7, 8	Bass or heavy trout; light salt water
9, 10, 11, 12	Heavy salt water

These three outfits—2-weight, 5-weight, and 10-weight—represent the range in fly-fishing gear, from ultralight trout to heavy salt water.

Devote the largest percentage of your budget to the rod. You can become an expert fly caster using an inexpensive reel or cheap waders, but a good rod is the piece of equipment that makes the most difference in how quickly and how well you learn to cast.

Rod Material

Graphite is overwhelmingly the best choice for fly rod material today. Graphite is pure carbon in its crystalline form. Material made from graphite fibers was first developed by the military in the 1960s to replace metal in applications such as aircraft design, where strength, hardness, and light weight were key features. Graphite has since become the material of choice in sporting equipment, including tennis rackets, skis, golf clubs, and fishing rods.

The first fly rods were made of wood, but they were heavy and lacked the quick action that's best for fly casting. In the mid-1800s, craftsmen began making rods of bamboo strips glued together to form a hexagonal shaft, a technique perfected by Hiram Leonard and Edward Payne in the 1870s. Until the late twentieth century, the best fly rods were bamboo, and some purists and veteran fly casters still prefer them for their feel and craftsmanship. However, good bamboo rods are very costly, are slightly heavier than graphite, require more practice to master, and offer no concrete advantages, with the possible exception of the ability to present a dry fly more delicately in the hands of an expert.

Fiberglass was the first synthetic fiber to be used with any success in fishing rods. It first appeared in fly rods in the 1950s, and the technology and manufactur-ing processes have improved greatly—in fact, they became the model for the processes used in making graphite rods. The only advantages of fiberglass rods over graphite are price and durability, but they lack the quick action and light weight of graphite rods.

In some top-of-the-line rods, boron is combined with graphite to produce a light, strong composite with a very fast action. Boron, which is extracted from the mineral borax, is too costly and difficult to work with to justify the slight advantage in weight and action it offers over graphite, so few manufacturers use it in their rods.

All graphite rods are not created equal, as you might guess from the fact that they range in price from $50 to $650. This disparity reflects the wide range not only in the quality of the material but also in the complexity of the design and manufacturing process. A $50 rod may be part graphite, part fiberglass and have sloppy action that makes basic casting a chore and precise casting impossible. Each rod manufacturer has proprietary materials, processes, and design specifications. A good rod is a combination of excellent materials and craftsmanship, and most brands have slightly different characteristics. In short, rod making is an art.

Rod Guides

Fly-rod guides are important. In studying catalog descriptions of fly rods, you'll see that most manufacturers mention them, and here's why. Their function is to keep the line shooting straight out along the rod during casts, not wasting energy by flapping around in other directions. Thus fly rods have more guides per foot than

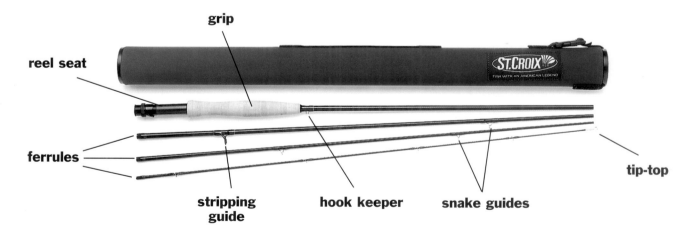

Four-piece pack rods, like this Reign model from St. Croix, have become very popular, as they can be stowed in a 30-inch tube for carrying ease. Modern ferrules are so lightweight, strong, and precisely engineered that the action of a four-piece rod is virtually the same as that of a traditional two-piece rod.

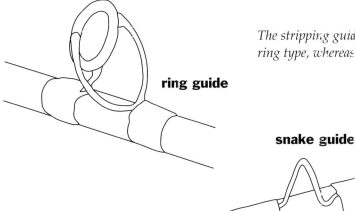

ring guide

snake guide

The stripping guide and tip-top guides of a fly rod are typically ring type, whereas all the guides in between are snake guides.

other types of rods. A typical 9-foot fly rod has eleven guides.

The guides at either end of the rod have special functions. The one at the bottom, called the stripping guide, receives extra friction because the line is pulled against it at an angle when you strip in line retrieving a fly and when you let out line while casting. The stripping guide on a good fly rod is lined with a hard material such as aluminum oxide, silicon carbide, titanium oxide, or ceramic. The guide at the top of the rod, called the tip-top, likewise receives more wear because of the angle of the line going out and coming in, but this guide must be very light so as not to affect the action of the rod tip. The tip-top typically is made of chrome-plated stainless steel. Its shape is also important, in that it must allow the fly line to run smoothly through without binding or catching.

Because fly rods are long and light and require so many guides, the middle guides should be lightweight. The snake guide, a thin spiral of stainless steel, is the preferred design for all the guides between the stripping guide and the tip-top. Snake guides add little weight—about half that of a ceramic guide—and thus do not impair the rod's action.

If you are considering a used rod, always inspect the guides—particularly the stripping guide and tip-top—for nicks or abrasion.

Grip

Fly-rod grips are almost always made of cork and come in a variety of shapes. You may find a particular shape more comfortable than another, but this is purely a matter of preference. Many medium to heavy rods (6–weight and up) are equipped with a fighting butt, a padded ball that can be held against your stomach when playing the fish.

A cigar-shaped grip with the reel seat at the base (left) is the most common style for rods up to 6-weight. Rods 8-weight and heavier typically have a Wells grip (flared at the top) and an extended butt section beneath the reel seat called a fighting butt. Both of the reel seats shown here are up-locking: the reel's forward foot fits into a lip at the base of the cork grip, and the reel is pushed forward (up) by rotating a ring at the base of the reel.

5

Gear

Reel Seat

The reel seat is the section of the handle to which the reel is attached. Its only function is to hold the reel securely to the rod. In most cases, it consists of a metal sleeve on which the reel sits and a locking mechanism to keep the reel securely fastened. On some expensive rods, where each piece of hardware is an aesthetic element, the reel seat may be made of an exotic hardwood or jewelry-grade nickel silver. But anodized aluminum does the job just as well.

Most reel seats today are the up-locking type, where the front foot of the reel fits into a slot underneath the grip, and a threaded ring is screwed up over the rear foot, pushing the reel up and snugly into place. The only differences in a down-locking seat are that the fixed slot is positioned at the bottom of the rod and the tightening screw is at the top of the reel seat.

Some light rods have sliding-ring seats, an old and very simple design in which a ring slides over each foot of the reel, holding the reel to the cork grip by friction. In a modified version, one foot of the reel slips into a hood at the top of the handle, and the other foot is fastened by sliding the ring onto it. Although sliding-ring systems look insecure, they actually work fine on 4-weight and lighter outfits and have the advantage of adding almost no weight to the rod.

Rod Length

Fly rods are longer than other types of rods, because in fly fishing the rod is more involved in the cast than in spinning or bait casting, where the weight of the lure pulls out the line. The typical spinning or casting rod is 6 or 6½ feet long, whereas most fly rods are between 8 and 9 feet long. In general, a longer rod is desirable in fly casting, because it provides a longer lever with which to keep the line in the air, waving back and forth over your head as you pay out line to reach your target. A longer rod is also an advantage when you need to pick up or reposition line already lying on the water, such as when you roll cast or lift a fly that's drifted past one fish and flick it toward another. This move is unique to fly fishing; with a spinning or casting rod, you have to reel in your line and cast again.

Shorter or longer fly rods are also available. Rods as short as 6 feet are made for casting tiny flies on 1-weight line and as long as 10 feet for 12-weight line and big saltwater gamefish. Two-handed rods may reach 15 feet. Other factors being equal, a longer rod will make longer, more efficient casts than a shorter rod.

Rods between 8 and 9 feet suit most fishing situations, however, and this is certainly the best range for learning to cast. Which length you should buy depends on your home water and your own size and comfort. If your home water is a small stream flowing through a brushy or heavily wooded valley, an 8-foot rod may be easier to handle because it is less likely to hit overhanging branches and brush on backcasts, and on such water, you probably won't need the extra distance of a longer rod anyway. You might even try a 7½-footer if casting conditions are really tight. However, if your stream is more open—if it flows through meadowland and is subject to wind—you would be better off with a 9-foot rod for the added distance and power. Also, most instructors recommend a 9-foot rod as the best length for learning to cast.

Action

A fishing rod's action is the way it flexes under tension. A rod flexes when you cast and retrieve a fly, and also when you play a fish. Good fly rods have what is called

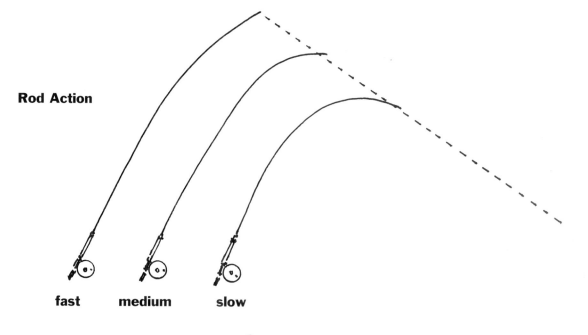

Rod Action

fast   medium   slow

a progressive taper: The tip is the most flexible, the midsection less so, and the butt section quite stiff.

Stiffer rods are said to have fast action because the tip snaps back to its original position very quickly after the power stroke of a cast or the pull of a fish. More limber rods are said to have slow action because they bend more easily when stressed and also bend farther down into the midsection of the blank, recovering more slowly.

In fly rods, more than any other type of fishing rod, the action is crucial to the cast. A rod that is too stiff for the line will not generate much line speed because it won't have any whip to it, and a too-stiff, too-fast tip will not give the angler enough feel or control over presentation of the fly. A rod that is too limber, however, doesn't have enough backbone to lift and propel the line. Of the various rod materials, fiberglass is the slowest, bamboo next, then graphite, with boron the fastest.

In choosing a fly-rod action, the trade-off is between the high line speed and greater distance attainable with ultrafast actions and the more precise control and casting ease of a slightly slower action. Experience, skill, type of fishing, and personal preference all are factors in choosing the action that is best for you, but a medium or medium-fast action is best for most situations and certainly the best for learning to cast.

Rod Recommendation

For your first outfit, buy an 8$\frac{1}{2}$- or 9-foot, medium-fast graphite rod from an established fly-rod maker in the weight most suited to your home water or type of fishing. Light- and middle-weight outfits—4-, 5-, or 6-weight—are easiest to master. Most established makers, including Sage, Loomis, and St. Croix, to name a few, make entry-level fly rods for between $100 and $200, and a few companies, such as Temple Fork Outfitters and Diamondback, specialize in rods of this price range. Another option is the store brand of one of the giant outdoor-sports retailers, Cabela's or Bass Pro Shops. Both have a line of fly-fishing equipment aimed at first-time or budget-minded buyers.

A midpriced rod may work just as well as an expensive one. In fact, it may be built from the same blank as a $500 rod, the only difference being the type of materials in the hardware and fittings. Choose wisely and you'll get a rod you'll have for the rest of your life, one that may even become a favorite in your final collection.

Do not buy a rod from a company that does not specialize in fly-fishing equipment, and avoid packaged starter outfits with rod, reel, and line for under $100, often sold at large sporting-goods retailers or in the fishing department of Wal-Mart. You may find a decent rod for $100, but not a whole outfit.

FLY LINE

The line is more essential to the cast in fly fishing than in spinning and bait casting, where the weight of the lure pulls out the line. In fly casting, the line itself is cast, and the nearly weightless fly just goes along for the ride. Therefore, fly line must be heavy enough to be propelled by the rod's casting motion alone. Also, the line's weight must be distributed along its length in a tapered profile so that the line shoots forward when cast and does not collapse in a heap when the rod stops in its forward position.

The first effective fly lines were made of silk and had to be dried and treated between fishing trips to restore their buoyancy. Modern lines are made of unsinkable polymers that can be molded into precise tapers and require just a quick cleaning between uses to keep them at peak performance. Do not balk at the expense of good fly line. It's absolutely worth the money and will last for many years.

Fly-Line Tapers

Most fly lines are thicker in the forward section, called the belly, to make them cast easier and farther. Level line is still available for trolling, but it is the worst choice for casting.

Weight-Forward. The weight-forward (WF) taper is the best for most fishing situations and also the easiest to learn how to cast. The first 30 feet of a WF line are thick, except for the very tip, where the fly line connects to the leader, and the back 60 feet are thin, level line.

Double-Taper. Before weight-forward lines were developed, the double-taper (DT) was the most popular, and many trout fishermen still prefer this design because they feel it gives them more control, particularly in mending line and roll casting. Double-taper lines also have an economical advantage: Because of their symmetrical design, when you wear out the forward section, you can reverse the line on your reel.

Specialty Tapers. Bass bug tapers were the first in the family of modified weight-forward lines that have a shorter, thicker belly than a conventional WF line. Designed to make long casts with large flies in windy conditions, they are sometimes called saltwater tapers. Many species-specific varieties are now on the market, including those for pike, bonefish, and tarpon. Whatever they are called, these lines all operate on the principle

Fly-line coding is standard among manufacturers. The label on the box indicates the line's taper, weight, and floating-sinking type, in that order. Thus, WF-5-F designates a weight-forward, 5-weight, floating line.

Fly-Line Tapers

━━━━━━━━━━━━━━━━━━ **level**

━━━━━━━━━━◄█►━━━━━━ **weight-forward (WF)**

◄━━━━━━━█████━━━━━━► **double-taper (DT)**

━━━━━━━█████━━━━━━━ **bass bug**

that a heavy, short front section will drive a big fly more effectively than a conventional line.

Floating and Sinking Lines

A floating line (F) is by far the easiest and, in most situations, the best type to use. Don't even consider anything else for your first line. Even when fishing underwater flies, such as nymphs, wet flies, and streamers, in most cases there is no need for the line to sink because the leader will sink far enough to get the fly down to the fish. And besides, you want the line to float. When making a new cast, you have to lift the line, usually twenty feet or more, off the water. If the line is underwater, you have to retrieve most of it before starting the next cast. If, on the other hand, the line is floating high on the surface, you can quickly and easily lift it by raising your rod. Yet another reason for using floating line is that it is easier to cast because it is less dense than sinking line and thus also "floats" in the air more readily than sinking line.

However, there are situations when you need a sinking line, namely, when the fish are deeper than the leader and fly will sink by themselves. This can occur in lakes, rivers, or any moving water where the current is fast enough to prevent a fly from getting down to the fish. The faster the current, the more weight is needed to get a fly down.

Unless the fish are very deep, a sinking-tip line is the best choice because it retains most of the casting and handling ease of a floating line. Only the front portion of such a line sinks and the rest floats, hence the code F/S for floating/sinking. The length of the sinking tip and the sink rate in IPS (inches per second) are given on the box. Sinking-tip lines are designated as Type I through VI; the higher the number, the greater the sink rate.

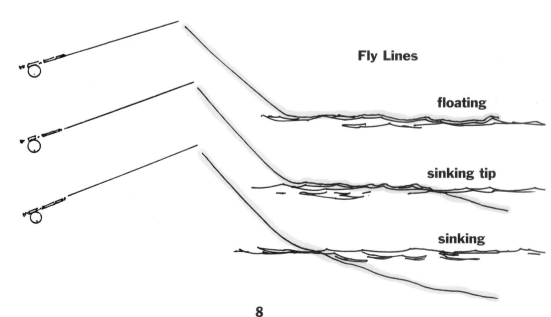

Fly Lines

floating

sinking tip

sinking

Other sinking lines available are full-sinking (S), for situations where the fish are very deep, and intermediate (I), which sink just below the surface.

Line Coding

Tapers:
> WF (weight-forward); DT (double-taper);
> L (level); ST (shooting taper)

Line types:
> F (floating); S (sinking);
> F/S (floating/sinking); I (intermediate)

Example:
> WF-5-F = weight-forward, 5-weight,
> floating line

Line Color

Why do fly lines come in such gaudy colors—lime green, bright yellow, pink? Simply to make them more visible to the angler. The fish don't care. In fact, some experts doubt that fish can discern colors at all, especially when the object is above them, backlit, and perceivable only in silhouette. Furthermore, the fly line is separated from the fly by 7 to 10 feet of thin, clear leader, so the fish can't connect it visually to the line.

For you, however, tracking the line will become second nature. You'll watch your casting loops in the air to diagnose the tempo of your stroke. You'll watch the head of the line just before it lands to make last-minute adjustments toward your target. You'll watch the line's curvature as it drifts to see if you need to mend line to prevent drag on the fly. And when nymph fishing, you'll watch the line for the slightest upstream twitch that may be the only clue a trout has picked up your fly.

So pick a color that's easy for you to see on the water where you fish.

Cleaning Line

Modern fly lines are well-nigh indestructible and, unlike their predecessors, do not need to be treated or dried to maintain their buoyancy. They do get dirty, however. As you fish, the line picks up grit and algae from the water, particles from backcasts that hit land or vegetation, and dirt and sand from loops that lie on the ground when you stop to tie on a new fly. It also picks up grease and dirt from your hands. A clean line slides through rod guides more easily, giving you longer casts with less effort, and it also floats higher. You'll be pleasantly surprised at the difference.

To clean your line, use the cleaning pad provided with some lines or a piece of cloth wet with line cleaner from a bottle. With one hand, pinch the line just above

Fly-line cleaner improves the performance of your line. A clean line shoots through rod guides more smoothly and also floats higher in the water.

Squeeze a small amount of cleaner onto a soft piece of cloth. Whenever you clean your line, whether at home or on the stream, stand on a surface that is free of dirt, sand, or other particles that might stick to the line when it falls to the ground.

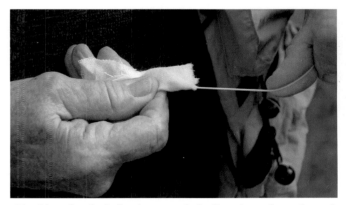

Pinching the cloth firmly around the line, just above the reel, strip off about 30 feet and let it fall to the ground. Then simply reel the line back onto your reel.

the reel with the pad or cloth, and with the other hand, grab the line above. Strip about thirty feet off the reel, pulling it through the pad or rag and making sure that the loose line falls on a relatively clean surface, such as the floor of your house, the bottom of the boat, or the surface of a stream.

BACKING

Fly line is only about 90 feet long, and a big fish that decides to make a long run can strip that length of line from a reel in no time. For this reason, the first thing you tie onto your reel is an appropriate length of Dacron backing line. The bigger the quarry and the heavier the reel, the more backing you'll need. Your reel specifications will say how much backing will fit on the spool with the fly line. A 4-weight reel typically takes 30 to 50 yards of backing, 5- to 8-weights between 100 and 150 yards, and big saltwater reels up to 300 yards. If you fish for average-size trout in small streams, you likely will never need backing, but why risk it? One of the most dramatic lines in a fly-fishing story is "He took me into the backing."

The length of backing you need depends on the capacity of your reel (check the box it came in) and the type of fishing you plan to do.

LEADERS

For trout fishers, the leader has more direct impact on fishing success than any other single piece of equipment—ironic, as it is the least expensive. Take this to heart, and always buy the highest-quality leaders you can find. If you're stuck buying leaders in the sporting-goods department of a large retailer, where choices are limited, always buy the most expensive type. Take an oath: Never, ever buy cheap leaders.

The leader is crucial because its function is to disguise the connection between you and the fly. A fine, transparent leader not only separates the fly visually from the thick fly line, but also, more significantly, allows the fly to settle on the water and drift naturally. If you were to tie your fly directly to the fly line, the counterfeit would be immediately obvious. For one thing, the fly line would put the fly down onto the water heavily at the end of the cast rather than letting it float down, as a delicate leader will. For another, the thick, buoyant fly line would drag the fly wherever it went on the water, whereas a thin leader sinks and will, with proper technique, let the fly float as if detached. Trout are keenly aware of everything that moves around them, particularly predators and food, and watch in-

sects drift by them all day long. They won't eat something that doesn't look edible, and they won't even consider something that behaves unnaturally. Thus the effect of a leader on the motion of a fly is perhaps more important than its invisibility. A trout probably isn't bothered by a wisp of monofilament on the water. It will, however, immediately reject an insect that is moving faster or slower than the current or sitting oddly in the film.

Good leader material is limp and strong. It does not have memory—it will not retain its coils after unfurled from the package—and it has high knot strength. Fly casting is tough on a leader. Positioned at the very end of the line, the leader is constantly being whipped through the air in tight loops. A cheap leader will develop kinks and bends, whereas a good leader will stay limp and kink-free.

To do its job in the casting and presentation of a fly, a leader must be tapered: thick at the butt end, where it attaches to the fly line, and very thin at the tip, where it attaches to the fly. This end section is called the tippet. Leaders are labeled with two dimensions: length and tippet strength. Most leaders range in length from $7^1/2$

to 12 feet and in tippet diameter from 8X, the thinnest, to 0X, the thickest.

In general, you want to use the shortest and strongest leader you can get away with. The more clear and still the water and the more spooky the trout (often related phenomena), the longer the leader you'll need.

The size of the fly dictates the tippet size (see table). Large and heavy or wind-resistant flies require thicker tippets, as delicate tippets will collapse under their weight, making it hard to put the fly right where you want it or set it down lightly on the water. Conversely, small flies cannot be presented naturally with a heavy tippet. If the leader material is too stiff, the fly goes where the leader does on the water rather than vice versa.

Knotted Leaders

Many fly fishers make their own leaders by knotting together several sections of monofilament. Each section is slightly thinner as you move from butt to tippet. Knotted leaders do have advantages, and some expert anglers swear by them. You can custom build them to your own specifications. Their segmented construction makes it convenient to change tippets on the stream. But perhaps most significant is that in the hands of a good caster, a knotted leader presents a fly a bit more smoothly than a store-bought tapered leader, turning over better at the end of the cast. Finally, in the long run, making your own knotted leaders is less expensive than buying packaged knotless leaders individually because monofilament, like everything else, is cheaper in quantity.

The disadvantage of a knotted leader is . . . the knots. A standard 9-foot trout leader consists of eight sections that require seven knots to connect. If you lack the patience, time, or skill for knot tying, or if you simply don't enjoy it, forget knotted leaders.

Knotless Tapered Leaders

For many fly fishers, and certainly for beginners, prepackaged leaders are a better choice than homemade knotted ones. Knotless tapered leaders are much more convenient and have no significant drawbacks in most situations.

A knotless leader tapers smoothly and progressively from butt to tippet, without the distinct separation between sections of a knotted leader. This leads to the one practical disadvantage of fishing with knotless leaders: Because of their gradual taper, you can't see where the tippet begins. To appreciate this issue, consider what happens to your tippet on a typical day on the stream: You clip off a little of your tippet each time you tie on a new fly, either when changing patterns or snapping off a fly on a snag. Say you're using a 9-foot 4X leader. The last 18 to 24 inches of such a leader is 4X diameter, after which the monofilament begins thickening. After a day of fishing, you may have cut off most or all of the tippet and be tying your fly to 6X material. At this point, you could replace the entire leader with a new one, but the better option, and the one most anglers use, is to carry spools of tippet material and tie on a new tippet when necessary.

But when is it necessary? Yes, the tricky part about changing the tippet on a knotless leader is recognizing

Tippet Specifications and Use

Tippet size	Diameter (in.)	Strength (lb.-test)*	Fly sizes
7X	.004	2	20–26
6X	.005	3	16–22
5X	.006	4.5	14–18
4X	.007	5.5	12–16
3X	.008	6.5	10–14
2X	.009	9	2–10
1X	.010	11	2–6
0X	.011	13	1/0–4

Leader material from different manufacturers varies slightly in test strength. The figures here are averages.

Knotless tapered leaders come in a variety of weights and lengths. Carry extras of the sizes you use most often.

when the majority of the original tippet has been cut off and figuring out where to attach the new one. If you've been clipping off a few inches over several hours, how do you keep track of how much tippet remains? Here's a trick: When you rig up, measure your leader against your rod. Conveniently, leaders are almost always close to the length of the rod, and sometimes exactly so. A common length for both rods and leaders is 9 feet. As you're fishing, you can easily check the leader against your rod to gauge how much tippet is left.

To summarize a leader system that works for many anglers: Buy a few knotless leaders in the sizes you use most often, along with spools of tippet material to match. Tie on a new leader at the beginning of the season, and then keep replacing its tippet as needed. Eventually you'll need to replace the whole leader, but it may last for many weeks.

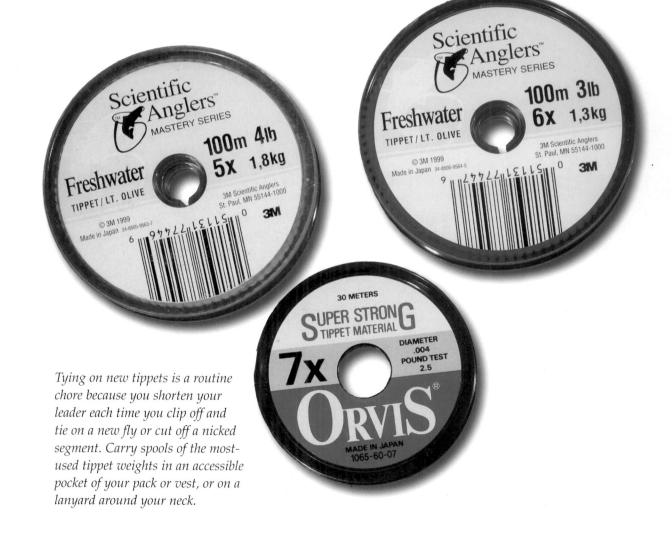

Tying on new tippets is a routine chore because you shorten your leader each time you clip off and tie on a new fly or cut off a nicked segment. Carry spools of the most-used tippet weights in an accessible pocket of your pack or vest, or on a lanyard around your neck.

12

A fly reel, in most cases, need not be expensive. Whereas casting and spinning reels are complex pieces of machinery, with gears and bearings crucial to casting and playing fish, a fly reel has few moving parts and does nothing during the cast or retrieve except store unused line. When playing fish up to a pound or so (15 or 16 inches), you don't even use the reel anyway, but bring in the fish the same way you retrieve a fly—by stripping in line by hand. The one situation where a more advanced reel is warranted is when playing large fish, in which case a good drag is essential.

Why, then, are there so many expensive fly reels on the market? In some cases the expense is justified, such as in saltwater reels, which must be corrosion-proof throughout and have strong, smooth drags for handling big, long-running fish. But a $300 reel for a 4-weight trout rod used on 12-inch trout? The honest answer is that some anglers who pay $500 for a rod simply want a nice piece of metal to attach to it.

Lightweight trout reels, like the 2-weight at left, need not have disc drags or large spools for holding a lot of backing. Medium-weight trout reels, like the 5-weight in the center, are now available with disc drags and large arbors, though a disc drag is not needed for average-size trout. For saltwater reels like the 10-weight, at right, however, a disc drag is a must, as is a large-capacity spool to hold at least 150 yards of backing.

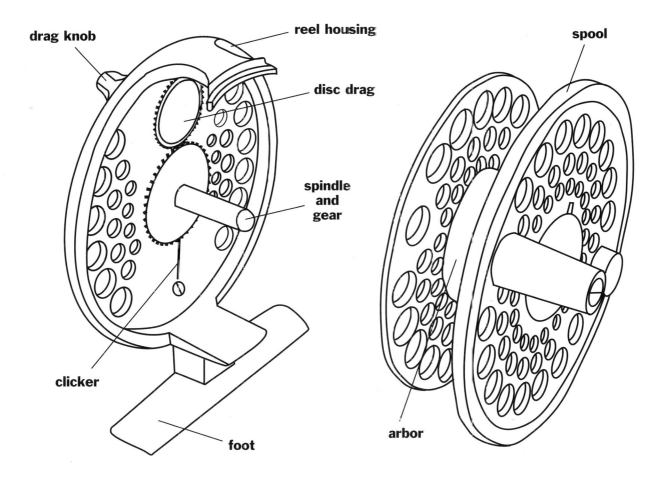

Parts of a single-action, small-arbor, disc-drag trout reel.

Drag

The drag on a fishing reel is a braking mechanism that slows the spinning spool against a fish pulling out line. A good drag is especially important when playing big fish on fly-fishing gear, because you're usually using a relatively light tippet. If your reel had no drag—if you tried to stop a fish cold by grabbing the reel handle—the fish would snap the tippet. The drag on a good fly reel can be set to the breaking strength of the leader.

The simplest and least inexpensive fly-reel drag is the click-and-pawl design: a metal tab that catches against a geared wheel. This ratchet device prevents the spool from rotating backward and can also slow the rotation of the spool if you increase tension on the tab by turning a knob on the outside of the reel, which controls a leaf spring that presses against the tab. A click-and-pawl drag is fine for most freshwater fishing. Its most basic function is to slow the spool enough to keep it from racing forward and causing tangles when you strip off line. If you do encounter a larger fish that you must play from the reel, the click-and-pawl drag will give you a bit of control . . . but not much. It won't slow down a really big fish.

For that, you'll want a reel with a disk drag, which works by applying pressure from a pad or set of pads against the spool itself. Disk drags are much more effective than click-and-pawl; they apply pressure more evenly and firmly and are more precisely adjustable. The wide range in cost of disk-drag reels reflects differences in design and materials. Drag pads and washers may be made from cork, felt, graphite, or stainless steel, and the entire drag system can be sealed to prevent moisture from entering, a key feature in saltwater fishing.

The rule of thumb is that the bigger the fish, the more important the drag.

Action

Most fly reels are single-action—one full rotation of the knob equals one rotation of the spool—and this design is fine for all but the largest and longest-running fish. Double-action reels have gearing that makes the spool rotate up to two times per turn of the handle, a feature that is useful for reeling in large fish that have taken out a lot of line.

Automatic reels are also available, but avoid them, as they are heavy and tend to be problematic. The only advantage to this design is the instant retrieval of loose line by pushing a trigger that releases a coiled metal spring inside the housing, making the spool spin rapidly in reverse.

Arbor Size

The arbor is the hub around which the line is wound. Traditional fly reels have small, narrow-diameter arbors.

The advantage to this design is that it leaves lots of room for line. The disadvantage is that when most of your fly line is out on the water, you have to do a lot of cranking to retrieve it, because one revolution of the spool gathers only a small amount of line. This extra cranking is just an annoyance when you're retrieving slack line, but it's more of a problem if you're playing a big fish from the reel. When you first start to crank the fish in, you don't get much line back at all. Only when you have enough line back on the spool to effectively increase the size of the arbor does your retrieve rate pick up.

A large-arbor reel solves this problem by substantially increasing the diameter of the hub onto which the line is wound, therefore increasing the amount of line retrieved on one handle crank.

Like a reel's drag, arbor size becomes more of an issue the larger the fish.

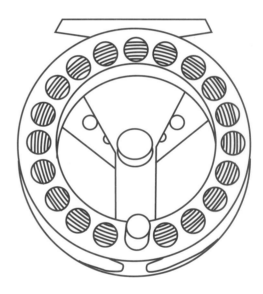

A large-arbor reel, because of its larger-diameter hub, retrieves more line with each revolution of the spool.

Spare Spools

Make sure whatever reel you buy accepts spare spools so you can keep different weights and types of lines, such as both sinking and floating, handy for changing at streamside or as situations arise. Spools are a lot cheaper than entire reels and less bulky to carry. Also, many reels are designed for two or more rod weights, and if you have spare spools, you can use the same reel frame on more than one rod by just swapping spools. At your fly shop, check out this feature of each reel you consider. You should be able to pop the spool off and on easily, and spares should be readily available to buy as needed.

Once you have the essentials—rod, reel, line, leaders, and some flies—you're ready to catch fish. But you will no doubt want some other gear as well. As you'll soon discover, the array of fly-fishing accessories is endless. What follows is a concise guide to the most useful.

Waders

Trout being a cold-water species, all trout fishers wind up buying waders. Except for shallow streams in the hottest months, the water in trout streams is just too cold for comfort.

Your first choice is between neoprene and a breathable fabric, like Gore-Tex. Neoprene is tough, heavy, warm, and considerably less expensive. If you're on a budget or fish mostly in cold, deep rivers, neoprene is a good choice. But after a few hot summers wading in neoprene, you'll be ready to invest in breathable waders, which are not only cooler, but also much lighter in weight. For the cold months, you can wear a pair of fleece wader liners or long johns underneath.

Waders also come in two foot styles: stocking-foot, which must be worn with wading boots, and boot-foot, which have the boots molded to the wader tops. Boot-foot waders are quicker to put on and take off. Stocking-foot waders with wading boots are much more comfortable, especially if you do a lot of walking to and from or along the stream when you fish.

Wading-boot soles are made of felt, rubber, or a combination of felt and metal studs. Felt is a good all-around choice for wading on most riverbeds, as it provides traction on slick rocks, the most common wading hazard. Cleated rubber soles are designed specifically for mud and gravel bottoms. Studded felt soles are for the toughest wading conditions: fast rivers with very

Felt-soled wading boots (rear) are the most popular all-around type because they prevent slipping on rocks, the most common hazard in trout streams. Studded soles (foreground), are designed to grip even the most slippery, algae-covered rocks, though they don't provide quite as much traction as plain felt on normal rocks, because not as much of the sole contacts the rock. Cleated rubber soles, also called lug soles, (not shown) are best if your wading is confined to mud, sand, or gravel bottoms.

Gaiters, or gravel guards, wrap around your ankles to keep small rocks and grit from slipping down into your wading boots.

Boot-foot waders (left) are quicker to put on, but stocking-foot waders with separate boots are more comfortable for walking and wading.

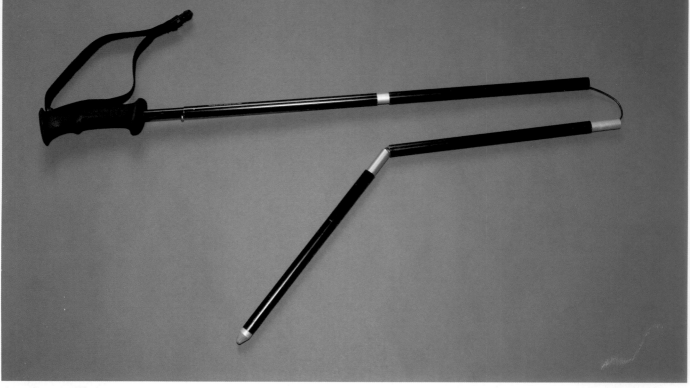

A wading staff helps prevent falls and could even save your life in fast, high water. A folding staff is handy: It fits in a scabbard on your belt and then snaps into position by itself when removed, leaving your other hand free to hold your fly rod.

slippery, algae-covered rocks. The studs actually grip the rock.

Make sure your wading boots come with gravel guards (gaiters), wide strips of material that wrap around your boot tops and fasten with Velcro. They prevent small stones from falling down between your boots and waders. Walking with stones in your boots not only is uncomfortable, but also can punch holes in the feet of your waders.

Most waders come with waterproof wading belts. When wading in deep, swift rivers, it's a good idea to wear this belt cinched above your waist to prevent your waders from filling with water should you fall down in the river—a potentially dangerous scenario.

Wading Staff

In fast rivers with rocky bottoms, a wading staff is just about a necessity and could even save your life. In less treacherous streams, it's just an annoyance that gets in your way and one more thing to carry.

The most convenient staffs are lightweight folding models, the sections connected by shock cord, like tent poles. Folded, the staff slips into a sheath carried on your wading belt. It snaps to full length when you pull it out and give it a shake.

You can also use an old ski pole or, the low-tech approach, a dead tree branch on the bank of the stream.

Fly Boxes

You'll need two types of fly boxes: one for dry flies and one for sinking flies (nymphs, wet flies, and streamers).

A dry-fly box has separate small compartments to hold flies without bending their hackle, the little fibers that radiate from the hook shank and keep the fly afloat. A dry fly that's been flattened won't float very well and won't imitate the insect it's designed to. The most expensive dry-fly boxes are aluminum, each compartment with its own clear plastic lid and spring-loaded hinge. Being able to open just one compartment has the practical advantage of preventing you from dumping all your flies if you should drop the box or turn it upside down. But any plastic box with compartments big enough to store your dry flies without damage is fine to begin with.

Boxes for sinking flies need not have individual compartments. Most have foam liners in which to embed the hooks and keep the flies in neat rows. As you collect more flies, you will want several of these boxes for flies of different sizes and types—one for small nymphs, one for large streamers, and so forth.

Good fly boxes are waterproof, with gaskets around their lids to create a tight seal. Moisture inside a fly box causes hooks to rust and, eventually, natural materials to deteriorate. This is why you shouldn't put a damp fly in the box. Let it dry first by hooking it in a fleece or foam patch on your vest.

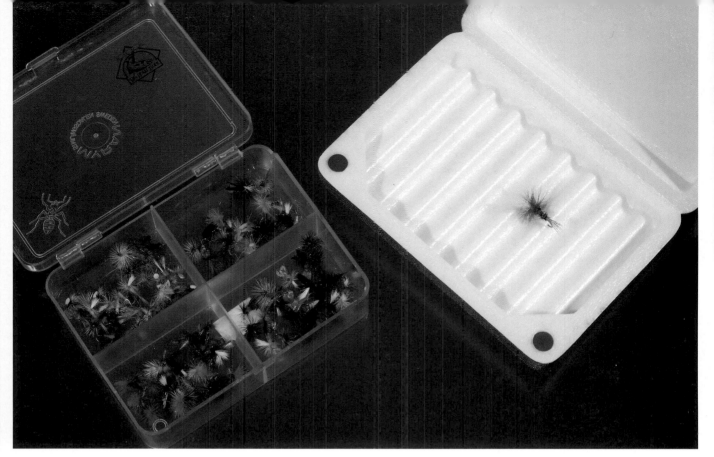

A dry-fly box must have compartments large enough that the flies' hackles and wings are not squashed when the lid is closed.

Boxes for underwater flies, such as nymphs and wet flies, can be slimmer than dry-fly boxes. The flies are stored by embedding the hooks in foam ledges.

Basic Gear Recommendations for Trout Fishing

Rod: 8¹/₂- or 9-foot graphite rod for 4-, 5-, or 6-weight line, depending on your home water, with medium or medium-fast action. Buy the best rod you can afford.

Line: Weight-forward (WF) taper, in 4-, 5-, or 6-weight, floating (F). Buy high-quality line.

Line Cleaner: Comes in small pads with fly line or separately in bottles.

Backing: One 100-yard spool of 20-pound-test Dacron backing.

Leaders: Several packs of 9-foot tapered, knotless leaders in 3X, 4X, 5X, and 6X, depending on the sizes and types of flies you'll be using. These cost about $3 each. Don't buy cheap leaders.

Tippet Spools: A spool each of 3X, 4X, 5X, and 6X tippet material, again depending on your needs.

Reel: Single-action. For most trout fishing, anything will work, but avoid automatic reels. If you're likely to be catching fish over two or three pounds regularly, a reel with disk drag and a large arbor is worth the extra money.

Waders: Stocking-foot waders and wading boots, with gravel guards and wading belt. Breathable fabric if you can afford it, neoprene otherwise.

Fly Boxes: One dry-fly box, one sinking-fly box.

Nippers: Carry these on a retriever.

Floatant: Buy a bottle on a harness that attaches to your shirt or vest.

Polarized Sunglasses: Use these once, even an inexpensive pair, and you'll never go fishing without them.

Vest or Pack: Whatever you choose need not be expensive but should be lightweight and comfortable, with enough pockets for at least two fly boxes and many small accessories.

Nippers

Changing flies is so much more convenient with a pair of line nippers that trout fishers don't go out on the stream without one. Keep your nippers on a zinger, a spring-loaded winder, pinned to your shirt pocket. Most fly-fishing nippers include a retractable point at one end that's used to poke dried head cement from the eye of a fly so you can thread your tippet through it.

Don't skimp on nippers. You'll use them constantly to change flies, and a cheap pair won't cut fine tippets cleanly. Most nippers come with a retractable needle for cleaning excess head cement from the eye of a fly so you can thread your tippet through it. (The pair above also has a knot-tying tool.) A spring-loaded retriever lets you clip the nippers to your shirt or vest for easy access on the stream.

Floatant

Floatant, a waterproofing liquid, is indispensable for dry-fly fishing. Dry flies gradually absorb water and lose their buoyancy as you fish them. Applying a thin film of floatant to the hackles keeps the fly riding high. Dry-fly fishers use floatant so regularly that they keep a bottle attached to the vest in a little harness.

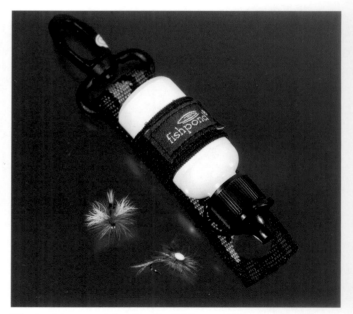

Floatant is a must for dry-fly fishing, as it keeps a fly riding high long after an untreated fly would become waterlogged. Buy a bottle with a little harness that attaches to your shirt or vest; this is one of these items you'll want close at hand.

A many-pocketed vest is traditional—and functional—garb for the fly-fisherman, as it keeps flies and tools within reach while wading.

Polarized sunglasses reduce surface glare on the water and are indispensable for spotting fish and following your fly as it drifts.

Many fly fishers prefer tackle packs to vests because they are cooler and more compact.

Polarized Sunglasses

Most fly casting is done in relatively shallow water and, whenever possible, to fish you can see. In fact, one of the sport's particular thrills is spotting a fish and delivering a fly to it with a well-placed cast. Polarized sunglasses are essential for spotting fish because they reduce the surface glare on the water. They also make wading safer by letting you see the bottom and avoid hazards like holes in the rocks or sudden drop-offs. And they protect your eyes from the sun and keep you from squinting all day.

All polarized sunglasses reduce glare, and even a pair off the rack in the drugstore will help you see beneath the surface of the water. Several companies make sunglasses specifically for anglers. They are much more expensive, but they generally have better lenses—more durable and of higher optical quality—and features like wraparound frames that block peripheral light. They come in a variety of lens colors for various fishing situations. Lenses in the brown or copper range are good for all-around freshwater fishing because they allow a bit more light to pass through than darker hues. They are therefore better for spotting fish and tying on flies in shaded streams or in the evening, any low-light situation where there's still enough glare on the water to make sunglasses useful.

Vest or Pack

Most trout anglers wade when fishing and need to wear something to carry their flies and accessories. The tradi-

Not all trout fishermen carry landing nets. A net does make landing fish easier, because it extends your reach—a handy feature when the fish is at the end of a long fly rod and a 9-foot leader—and also lets you contain a fish while you unhook it. On the other hand, if you practice catch-and-release with barbless hooks, you can easily release most fish with a tug on the hook and without lifting them from the water. Also, a net tends to snag on branches when you're walking through the woods.

tional garment is the fishing vest, which has lots of pockets. Another option is the fanny pack, which straps around your waist and is a bit less cumbersome and cooler in hot weather. Necklaces are also available onto which you clip your nippers, small tools, floatant, and so on. For those who carry a large assortment of flies, there are multiple fly-box systems that hang around your neck and fold down.

The simplest solution is an inexpensive fanny pack large enough to hold a few fly boxes, extra spools of tippets, and your fly reel. You can hang the rest of your paraphernalia on your shirt.

2

Knots and Rigging Up

Rigging a fly-fishing outfit requires more knots than rigging a spinning or bait-casting outfit. You must tie the line not only to the reel and lure, but also to the backing at one end and the leader at the other. And you must routinely tie new tippets to your leader. If you choose to make your own knotted leaders, the number of knots you tie will increase geometrically.

Entire books are available on fishing knots. This chapter presents six time-tested, reasonably simple knots that may be all you'll ever need.

As a general rule, moisten all knots with saliva before tightening them. Lubrication allows a knot to be cinched more tightly with less abrasion and stress, thus strengthening it.

"Tag end" refers to the short, working end of the line. "Standing line" refers to the portion of the line that goes toward the reel or spool of line.

ARBOR KNOT: BACKING TO REEL

The arbor knot is used to fasten the tag end of the backing to the reel so you can crank the rest of the backing onto the reel. It is a very easy knot to tie and is rarely stressed when fishing, because once you've attached the fly line to the backing and cranked it all onto the reel, the arbor knot is buried under a few hundred yards of line. It need only be snug enough in the beginning to let you begin winding the backing onto the reel.

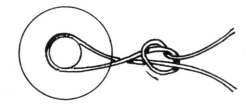

1. Loop the tag end of the line around the reel arbor, leaving about 6 inches extending. Tie an overhand knot around the tag end, but leave enough line extending from this knot to tie a second overhand knot at the very tip.

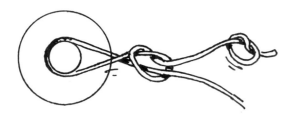

2. Tie a second overhand knot in the tag end. This prevents the tag end from slipping through the first overhand knot when you cinch the arbor knot tight against the spool.

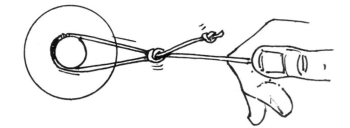

3. Moisten and tighten the two overhand knots. Trim any excess off the last knot. Holding the reel in one hand, pull the standing line with the other hand to draw the arbor knot snug.

NAIL KNOT: FLY LINE TO BACKING

The nail knot's virtue is that it creates a strong, smooth connection between two lines of different diameters: the thin backing and the thick fly line. A well-tied nail knot slides through the rod guides without catching, a feature you'll appreciate if a big fish strips all your line from the reel, and also lies flat on the reel, providing a smooth bed for the fly line wound over it.

The original method for tying this knot involved a nail, hence the name, but a hollow tube such as a three-inch length of plastic straw works better.

It may take a few tries to get the feel for this knot, especially keeping the winds intact when you remove the tube and cinch the knot tight, but even clumsy knot tiers can do it with some patience.

1. Lay the backing (top) and fly line on a bench top alongside the tube, with the tag end of the backing pointing left and the tag end of the fly line pointing right.

2. Bring the tag end of backing over the fly line and tube and start it up the near side.

3. Wind the backing to the right, around both tube and fly line, in seven closely spaced loops.

5. Holding the knot in place with your right thumb and forefinger, push the tube to the left and off the tag end of the backing.

4. Insert the tag end of the backing through the right end of the tube and push it all the way through, leaving a few inches extending out the left side of the tube. The basic knot is now formed; the next step is to keep it intact while you remove the tube and cinch the knot tight. Before moving to step 5, hold the knot loosely between your right thumb and forefinger, and pull gently on the tag end of the backing to snug the loops around the tube. Leave them loose enough that the tube can be slid out.

6. Tighten the knot by pulling the tag ends of the backing and fly line in opposite directions. Trim the ends close to the knot, leaving no ends protruding to catch on the rod guides.

SURGEON'S LOOP: LEADER TO FLY LINE, PART 1

The surgeon's loop is a fast, simple, effective way to make a loop in the butt end of a leader so it can be attached to the fly line with a loop-to-loop connection.

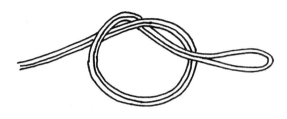

1. Double the butt end of the leader and make an overhand knot.

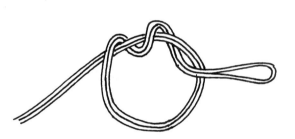

2. Bring the tag end of the loop over and under the standing portion to form a second overhand knot. Position these overhand knots so that when tightened, you'll be left with a loop about half an inch long.

3. While holding the overhand knots in place with one hand, pull on the standing portion to tighten the knots. Trim the excess.

LOOP-TO-LOOP CONNECTION: LEADER TO FLY LINE, PART 2

This connection requires a fly line with a loop in the end. Many lines are made this way, but if the brand you buy has a plain end, you can create a loop a number of ways. One is to affix a slip-on loop, available at fly shops or from fly-fishing catalogs, to the end of the fly line. Another is to tie a surgeon's loop in the end of the fly line, although this results in a bulky knot that catches in the guides.

To connect the leader and fly line, simply push the surgeon's loop at the butt end of the leader through the fly-line loop, and then thread the tip of the leader back through the leader loop, pulling on the tip until the two loops interlock. Before you pull the connection snug, make sure the leader loop does not flip over and form a girth hitch, which is a much weaker connection than a proper loop-to-loop.

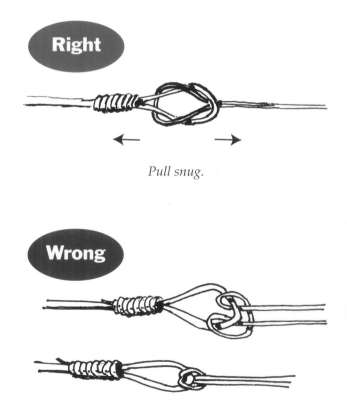

Don't let the loops flip over into a girth hitch as you pull the loops together. This is a very weak connection.

24

The surgeon's knot, simple, quick, and strong, is great for attaching a new tippet section to an existing leader. This is a routine procedure on the trout stream, because your tippet is gradually shortened each time you clip off to tie on a new fly or remove a segment that has been nicked by fish or snags. Also, you'll often have to switch to a heavier or lighter tippet when changing the type or size of fly.

1. Lay the leader and tippet on top of each other, facing in opposite directions and overlapping a few inches.

2. Tie an overhand knot in the doubled strands.

3. Tie a second overhand knot.

4. Moisten the knot and pull it snug, then pull on each of the four strands to make sure the knot is securely tightened.

5. Trim the two tag ends, double-checking first to make sure you're cutting the tag ends and not the leader itself. When you're working with a thin tippet in low light, it's easy to cut the leader by mistake.

The improved clinch knot is probably the most popular for tying on a fly, and for good reason: It's quick, simple, and strong. These features are significant. If you change flies often, you won't abide a knot that is hard to tie. But it needs to have great strength and must not slip, because you will exert direct pressure on it when playing and landing fish.

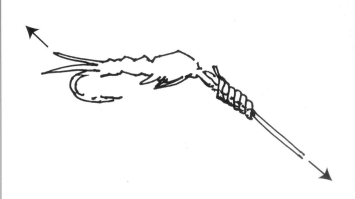

1. Thread a few inches of tippet through the eye of the fly, twist the tag end five or six times around the standing part of the line, and push the tag end back through the loop near the eye.

3. Moisten the knot and finish tightening it by gripping the fly at the bend of the hook with your left hand and pulling to the left while pulling the standing portion of the line to the right. Trim the excess.

2. Bring the tag end back through the loop just created, and then begin to tighten the knot by pulling the tag end an inch or two through this loop. A common problem is that the tag end slips back through the second loop as you tighten the knot. This is why you must leave a sufficient length of tag end protruding.

Knots and Rigging Up

Rigging up a fly-fishing outfit is easy, but here are a few tips to remember and some common mistakes to avoid.

- When gearing up at the car, put your waders on last. Rigging your rod and tying on flies is more comfortable in street clothes.

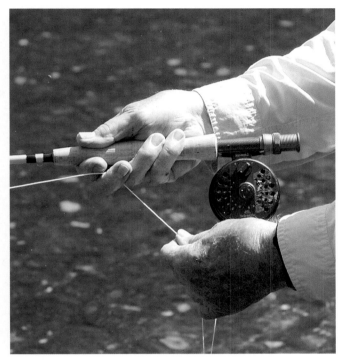

When rigging up, make sure you mount the reel with its handle on your line-hand side (for example, on the left side if you're right-handed).

- Mount the reel with the handle on your reel-hand side. If you're a right-handed caster, the reel handle should be on the left so you reel forward to retrieve line. It's easy to mount the reel backward, simply because a fly reel, unlike a spinning or bait-casting reel, has no obvious front and back—it's circular—and also because the handle is inconspicuous. I have more than once hooked a fish and then grappled for a reel handle that was not there.

To string your rod, double the fly line a foot or so behind the leader connection and pull the doubled line through all the guides, letting the leader follow behind.

- Thread the doubled fly line, not the leader, through the rod guides. Before beginning to thread your rod, pull the entire leader through the forward opening in the reel or through the oval line guard, if the reel has one, and let it fall to the ground. Then double the fly line at a point right behind the leader and push it through the guides, letting the leader follow along. If you thread the leader first and inadvertently let go when passing it through a guide, as often happens, the heavy fly line drags the light leader back through all the guides, and you have to start all over again.

- Don't miss a rod guide. Because fly rods are long and have many closely spaced guides, it's easy to miss one when you're rigging up. You may not notice this until you're in the middle of the stream and

Knots and Rigging Up

not getting the distance you expect from your casts, at which point you'll have to wade ashore, cut off your fly, and rerig the whole outfit. If you find yourself making this mistake, count the guides on your rod and tick them off as you rig your line each time.

- Tie on your fly and catch it in the hookkeeper at the base of your rod. In cases where your leader is longer than your rod, you'll have to reel the leader-fly line knot back through the tip-top guide when you crank the line snug. This can be a nuisance when stripping out line for your first cast, because the knot may not slip smoothly through the tip-top. A trick to avoid this: When rigging up, hook your fly onto your stripping guide instead of the hook-keeper, leaving a few feet of slack leader; then loop this slack around your reel frame and crank until the line is snug. This trick allows you to keep the line-leader knot outside the tip-top guide.

- When packing up at the end of the day, or after tying on a new leader or tippet at home, don't

crank the tippet all the way back onto the reel; leave a few inches dangling. On some reels, you can stick this tag end through one of the holes in the side of the spool, leaving an inch or two protruding. The tag end is then easy to find when you next rig up. If you reel the tippet completely onto the spool, it can get buried between the fly line and you'll have to dig it out, a chore that's especially maddening with fine tippets.

Murphy's Law of Rigging Mistakes
Each rigging mistake has a potential consequence, and the mistake you make on a particular day will always have that particular consequence. Thus if you put your reel on backward, you are destined to hook a 3-pound trout that requires your immediate access to the handle. If at the end of the previous trip you reeled your 7X tippet all the way onto your reel and buried it in your fly line, you will have to dig it out on an evening when the fish are rising everywhere, the light is failing, and the mosquitoes are out in hordes.

3
Casting

Fly casting requires more skill and dexterity than casting with spinning or bait-casting gear, but anyone can learn it well enough to catch fish, and most people find that handling a fly rod is a big part of fly fishing's appeal.

The fundamental difference between fly casting and conventional spinning or bait-casting tackle is that here you're casting the line, not the lure. With conventional tackle, the line is coiled on the reel when the cast begins, and when you whip the rod forward and release the line, the momentum of the forward-shooting lure pulls the line off the reel. When fly casting, you're pitching the line itself, so you have to learn some basic principles of the casting motion, namely, how to move and stop the rod so the line stays aloft and propels the fly where you want it to go.

Lefty Kreh's name has become synonymous with casting technique, not only because he is a renowned caster, but also because he's analyzed the fundamentals so thoroughly that he's been able to discard rigid traditional instruction and replace it with principles that are both easy to understand and adaptable to casters of any size, strength, or skill level. Lefty emphasizes that his principles are not rules he made up, but observations about how a fly line responds to the motion of a fly rod based on fundamental laws of motion. He stresses that understanding basic principles, rather than following rigid prescriptions for casting steps, allows you to adapt your technique to your own body type and ability. Rather than copy someone else's style, first understand how the fly rod works and then create your own style.

Lefty's Four Principles

Principle 1. Begin a forward casting stroke just as the line straightens behind you.

You cannot make an effective fly-casting stroke until you can make the fly—that is, the end of the line—move. If you begin a stroke with the line still furled, whether the furls are lying on the water or forming loops in the air, you'll make a sloppy and ineffective cast, because the first effect of your stroke will be to pull the curves out of the line, not move the end of the line. So whether you're picking up the line off the water to initiate a cast or false-casting back and forth in the air, don't begin a stroke until the line has almost entirely unfurled. Experienced casters can feel this moment without having to watch the line; they sense the rod tip loading as the line straightens. It's helpful to watch your line on both forward casts and backcasts, however, and Lefty recommends that you *start the stroke an instant before you see the line straighten.* If you wait until you actually see it straighten, your stroke will be a beat late, because it takes your brain an instant to process the visual cue and translate it into an arm motion.

Wrong

A stroke that begins too soon—as here, while the line is still furled—is inefficient, because it does not move the end of the line (and your fly) anywhere.

Casting

30

Principle 2. A casting stroke should speed up at the very end and stop abruptly.

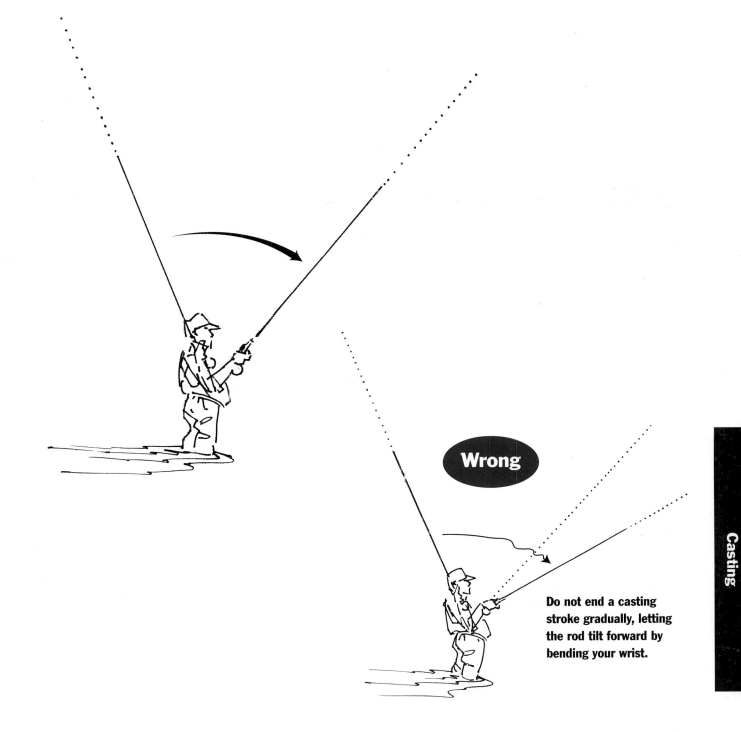

Wrong

Do not end a casting
stroke gradually, letting
the rod tilt forward by
bending your wrist.

End each casting stroke with a speedup and stop. The stroke should begin smoothly, gradually accelerate, and then—in the final fraction of its arc—accelerate sharply and stop dead. This is the most crucial and subtle skill in casting, and it is one of Lefty's great contributions to casting technique. Watch Lefty cast, and you're struck by the effortlessness of his motions. Look closer, and you'll see that although most of his casting motion is fluid, almost casual, the very end of each stroke is quick and crisp, and his rod stops dead. The shorter and swifter this stroke-ending motion, the tighter the loop and the more distance you get with less effort.

Principle 3. The line will go in the direction the tip is moving when the rod stops, whether on a backcast or forward stroke. A rod tip that stops at position 1, above, will propel the line level with the water. A rod tip that doesn't stop until it's moving downward, as in 2, will send the line downward, which makes for an inefficient cast. Even experienced casters are often unaware of the path of the rod tip, concentrating instead on the lower part of the rod.

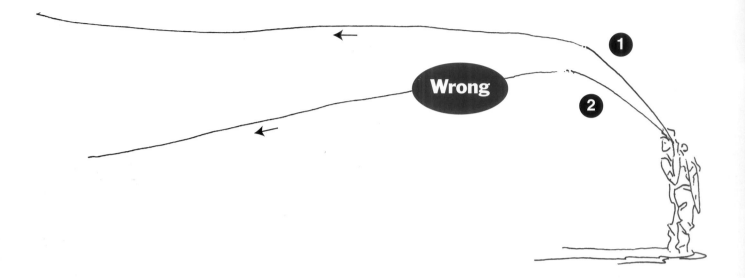

The line will go in the direction the rod tip is moving when it stops. This seems obvious, but beginners concentrating on their arm motion are often unaware of the position of the rod tip when a stroke ends. Thus they routinely drop the rod tip at the end of a stroke, sending the line downward when it should be shooting out level with the water or at a slight upward angle. Remember, then, it's not where you stop your arm but where you stop the rod tip that determines the direction in which the line will travel—up, level, or down.

Principle 4. For short casts, a short stroke is often sufficient. For longer casts with heavy flies or in windy conditions, lengthening the arc of your stroke will get you more distance with less effort.

The farther the rod travels between the backward and forward strokes, the less effort required to make the cast. This directly contradicts the traditional clock-face instruction, which strictly prescribes a casting arc that begins at ten o'clock and stops at one o'clock. Lefty emphasizes that the rod is like a lever, and the longer the arc through which a lever moves, the more work it can do with less force. Therefore, if you need to make a long cast or have to cast a heavy fly or any fly into the wind, lengthen your stroke. Conversely, when making short casts with a small trout fly, a short stroke is all that's necessary.

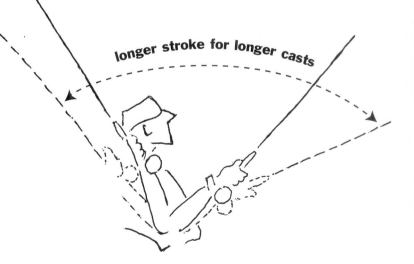

The following guidelines apply to all casts. They require no skill or dexterity, but if you train your arms and hands to move as described, you'll get better results with less effort.

Feet

Point the foot opposite your casting arm (your left foot if you're right-handed) toward the target, just as when throwing a ball. This orientation allows your torso to rotate naturally as your arm moves back and forth during casting strokes.

Arms

Keep your wrist straight, in line with your forearm, throughout the cast.

Bending your wrist on forward and back strokes creates wide, sloppy loops.

Keep your wrist in line with your forearm while casting. As you move the rod back and forth, pivot at the elbow and not the wrist. Casting with your wrist not only is tiring, but also creates wide, circular loops in the line rather than the tight loops of an efficient cast.

Don't lift your elbow on the backcast and lower it on the forward stroke. It should travel in a relatively straight line, as if it were sliding back and forth on a shelf mounted beside you a little above waist level.

Note how Lefty's elbow stays at waist level—"on the shelf"—throughout the entire casting stroke, a movement that helps produce tight loops.

Hands

For optimum control and ease of casting, hold the rod with your thumb at the back of the grip.

Wrapping your thumb around the grip reduces control of the casting stroke by making it harder for you to stop the rod crisply.

Hold your rod with your thumb at the back of the rod grip and maintain this orientation throughout the entire casting sequence. Keep your thumbnail pointed at the target during the forward stroke, and don't twist your wrist as you move the rod forward and back.

Extending your forefinger on the grip restricts your casting motion.

First, get about 30 feet of line out in front of you—which may be challenging, because you haven't learned to cast yet. If you're on the lawn, strip some line off your reel and walk backward until you have 30 feet or so lying on the grass in front of you. If you're wading in a stream, strip 30 feet off your reel and let the current take it downstream. If you're on the bank of a pond or stream, well, just flail around until you get some line out there. Heck, you might even learn to cast in the process. There are four steps in the casting sequence: pickup, backcast, forward stroke, and drop.

Step 1. Pickup

The first stroke in a forward cast sequence is the backcast, but many backcasts are doomed before they begin by faulty pickups. The key is beginning the stroke at the right moment, neither too soon nor too late.

With the line lying on the water or grass in front of you, grasp it at a point between the reel and stripping guide with the thumb and forefinger of your line hand (the left hand for right-handed casters).

Then lift your rod steadily until all the bends are pulled out of the line, the leader is just starting to come up off the surface, and the fly is just beginning to move. (Remember Lefty's first principle.)

This is the moment to begin your backcast. The line draped from your rod is pulling against the rod tip, flexing, or loading, it for the stroke to come, and enough line is off the water that you can get it and your fly neatly into the air. If you start the backcast too soon, you'll have to rip line off the water. But you can also make the opposite mistake, waiting too long to start the backcast. If your pickup motion is too long and slow, the line will have begun to sag down toward you by the time you start the stroke, and your backcast will never get cleanly launched.

The key, as in dating, is to wait until the right moment, and then make a brisk pickup.

The goal of the backcast is to unfurl the line behind you in prime position to be propelled forward in the forward stroke. Start your backcast at the pickup point described above, bringing the rod back smoothly and briskly—not too slowly, but not with a jerk either—to lift the line into the air. Gradually accelerate the stroke until, at the very end, you speed it up and then stop dead. You want to stop the rod at a point that will make the line shoot out behind you at a slight upward angle.

Remember Lefty's third principle: The line will go in the direction the rod tip is moving when it stops. Thus if you bring the rod tip too far back, a common mistake, the line behind you starts to fall before you can begin your forward stroke.

Likewise, if you don't stop the rod abruptly at a definite point on the backcast but let it keep drifting back until you start forward again, the line will not have unfurled behind you and will plow into itself when you get around to that forward stroke.

Casting

Watch your backcast and begin your forward stroke just before the line straightens out behind you. This is the same principle you used on the backcast: waiting until the rod loads before beginning the stroke. Following the backcast with your eyes means looking over your shoulder, not the most comfortable or efficient posture, but finding the right timing is more important. Soon you'll be able to get this timing without looking back: You'll feel the tension on the rod tip when the line straightens out.

Bring the rod forward crisply, and stop it dead at about the same place you began your backcast. Again, the timing of this stroke is more important than anything else. If you start forward too soon, the first effect of the forward motion will be to snap the bend out of the line, like cracking a whip. In fact, an audible crack is a telltale sign you're starting too soon.

Just as in the backcast, accelerate your stroke, speeding up and stopping dead at the end. The stopping point again is crucial. You want to stop the rod dead at a point where the line will shoot out level with the water—or at a slight upward angle—at about the height of your rod tip. The most common error is stopping too late, when the rod tip has begun to move down.

Casting

37

After this last abrupt stop, the casting sequence is over. Wait a beat until the line straightens out over the water and begins to fall—not before—and then slowly drop your rod tip, following the fly as it floats down through the air to the surface. Note that if you smush together the forward stroke and the drop—that is, if you don't stop your rod crisply but let it drift down toward the water after your forward cast—the line and fly will be pushed down onto the water with a splash, rather than being allowed to drift down and alight on the surface. This final touch of the cast directly affects your fishing, especially when presenting a dry fly to picky trout.

Lefty has devised a simple drill that you can do on a lawn to help you learn the rod motion necessary for tightening loops. You'll need two 50-foot lengths of rope (clothesline works fine) with a stake or large nail tied to each end of both. Lay out the ropes on the lawn, parallel to each other and about 4 feet apart, and pin them down. The object of the drill is to make individual back and forward strokes with your fly line such that it always lands between the two ropes—in other words, to develop a stroke that will produce tight loops.

Stand at the midpoint of the parallel ropes, facing them and back far enough from the near rope so that your rod tip, when rested on the ground in front of you, extends about a foot over the near rope. Strip out about 25 feet of line and position it to your left or right, between the two ropes.

With the line lying on the ground to your right or left, lift your rod so the tip is a foot off the ground, and then make a backcast (imagine you're making a sidearm cast on the water), letting the line fall to the ground at the end of the stroke. Note where the line falls. If you stop within the correct range, the line will fall between the two ropes. If you stop the stroke too far back, the most common error, the line will cross over the near rope.

Now do a forward stroke, trying again to keep the line between the ropes. Repeat this drill several times, stopping at the end of each stroke and noting where the line lands. When you're consistently putting the line between the ropes, you're casting with a motion that produces tight loops. Enough practice will cause this motion to be committed to muscle memory by the time you hit the water.

Begin with the line lying on the ground to your right, between the ropes.

Stop the rod in a position that lets the line fall to the grass between the ropes.

Make a forward stroke, as in a sidearm cast.

Now do the same drill for your backcast. Starting with the line on your left, make a backcast so that the line lands between the ropes to your right.

Good Pickup Form | ## Incorrect Pickup Form

1. The angler here is slowly lifting his rod but has not started his backcast because the forward portion of the fly line is still lying on the water.

2. Here he's lifted all the fly line off the water and is starting the backcast.

3. The backcast has begun. Note how the line lifts cleanly off the water with no splash.

The above sequence illustrates a common mistake—beginning a backcast too soon. With a long length of fly line on the water, the angler begins to lift his rod but starts his backcast well before all the line is lifted. Ripping line off the water (note the spray around the line) is noisy and inefficient. It wastes energy that should go into propelling the line rearward in the air and scares the fish.

Casting

Fly line unfurls as it travels through the air after a casting stroke. As Lefty says, "You don't cast a fly line, you unroll it." A *loop*, in fly casting, is the curvature of the leading section of line in the air. A tight loop is one in which the top and bottom are close together, a desirable shape because a flatter, more compact loop goes farther with less effort than a wider, more circular loop. Think of a tight loop as a bullet head shooting toward its target. Even very experienced casters, like golfers, tinker with stroke mechanics to tighten their loops.

The most common flaw in beginners' form is overly wide loops, which are usually caused by dipping the rod tip too far back at the end of the backcast or the forward stroke, instead of ending each stroke crisply with a speedup and stop. But wide loops are not a disastrous flaw. They will still allow you to cast a reasonable distance and present a fly fairly well. Rather than being obsessed with loop size at the start, you're better off getting comfortable enough with the casting motion that you can routinely put 30 or 40 feet of line out on the water. After you get the basic cast down, you can begin concentrating on loop size.

The keys to producing tight loops are posture, keeping your forearm and wrist in line and elbow on the shelf, and stroke timing, beginning your stroke at the right moment and—most important—ending it with a short, fast speedup and stop.

Casting

The loop on this forward cast is tight and efficient, the result of a short, crisp, speed-up-and-stop at the end of the forward stroke. The dotted line shows the shape of an inefficient wide loop, which can be caused by dipping the rod at the end of the backcast or forward stroke (often by bending your wrist), or by bringing the rod to a slow, gradual stop at the end of the stroke.

A tailing loop occurs when the leader, coming from the rear, plows into the forward section of the line during the forward stroke, making a mess of the final portion of the cast. It is, in effect, a loop that is too tight. This problem often develops when a caster tries to achieve tighter loops and greater distance by pushing the rod forward at the end of the forward stroke, rather than stopping it dead, or by accelerating the stroke too soon, rather than speeding up right at the end.

Lefty and his longtime fishing friend Ed Jaworowski, author of *The Cast* and *Troubleshooting the Cast*, suggest a subtle change in form that may eliminate tailing loops. First, make sure you're stopping the rod dead at the end of the stroke, not pushing the handle forward. But if tailing loops persist, try this: The instant after you stop the rod on your forward stroke, press down on the rod handle with your thumb, cocking your wrist slightly forward and causing the rod tip to dip just enough to allow the oncoming line to sail over—rather than plow into—the forward part.

Casting

A tailing loop, a common flaw, occurs at the end of a forward stroke, when the end of the line—rather than rolling out cleanly and dropping the fly on the water—plows into the forward part, often causing the fly to catch on the line and making a tangled mess.

When fishing, you will at times make a forward cast with just one backcast and one forward stroke. In most situations, however, you'll have to do some false casting—casting the line back and forth without letting it drop. You false-cast for three reasons: to shoot out more line, reposition the line on the water, or dry off a fly.

Getting Line Out at the Start

When letting line shoot out on a forward stroke, let it pass through an O formed with your thumb and forefinger.

The first thing you have to do when you arrive at your fishing spot is get enough line out to make your first cast. Pull a few feet of line through the top guide to get you started. Then strip several yards of line off your reel and let the coils lie in the water or on the ground. With the thumb and forefinger of your line hand, grasp the line at a point between your reel and the stripping guide, as you did when practicing the forward cast. When you want to shoot out line on your forward stroke, you'll modify this pinch grip into an O so the line can pass through.

Shooting Line

Now begin false-casting and shooting out line. Do a series of backcasts and forward strokes without letting the line fall to the water, and each time you stop the rod in the forward position, release the line with your line hand and let it shoot out through the O formed by the thumb and forefinger of your line hand. The momentum of the line going out will pull some of the coiled line along with it.

Line-Hand Control

The timing and technique of the line release are important. Don't release the line with your line hand until you feel the tug of the line straightening out in front of you. Releasing too soon—before the line has straightened—kills the momentum of the cast and decreases its distance.

If you release the line with your line hand as it shoots out, it will fall to your feet and reduce the distance of your cast.

Also, don't drop the line with your line hand when you release it; make the O described above. If you just let the line go, it will flap around on its way to the stripping guide, and you'll lose some distance on your forward cast. The most direct path the line can take between the reel and stripping guide, the better. In effect, your line hand becomes another rod guide.

When the line straightens in front of you and you're about to start a backcast, pinch it again with your line hand. Never release line on the backcast.

Starting from scratch, it will take a few sets of backcasts and forward casts to get 30 or 40 feet of line in the air. Note that the timing of these cycles changes as the length of line increases. At the start, when you have only a few yards out, your casting motion will be like waving the rod back and forth with hardly a pause. As the line lengthens, you'll have to pause a little longer at the end of each casting stroke to let the line straighten behind and in front of you.

Avoid the beginner tendency to false-cast more than necessary. Once you have enough line out to reach your target, drop the fly. It's tempting to false-cast just for the fun of it, just to enjoy your newfound command of the line. But it wastes energy and can scare fish. Veteran anglers tend to be economical in their casting, putting the fly where they want it with no wasted motion. They false-cast for only specific reasons: when they need to shoot out more line, are changing the direction of the cast, or need to air-dry a dry fly that's become soggy.

Casting

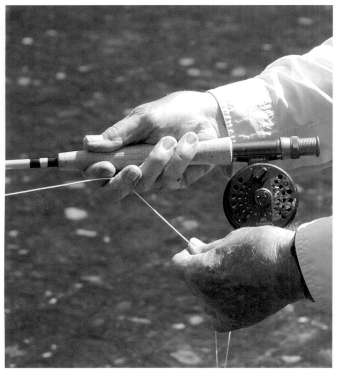

When stripping in line, guide the line between the first two fingers of your rod hand and pull down with your line hand.

Stripping Line. Retrieving line is a regular part of casting and fishing, whether to eliminate slack before the pickup of a cast, retrieve a fly in lifelike twitches, or bring in a fish. Most of the time, you retrieve line by stripping it in with your line hand rather than using your reel. To do this, guide the incoming line between the forefinger and middle finger of your rod hand and just pull straight down with your line hand. Your rod hand keeps tension on the line coming in and keeps slack from forming.

The sidearm cast is just a variation of the forward cast in which you hold the rod at an angle rather than in a vertical position. Visualize the difference between a sidearm and overhand delivery in pitching a baseball. The sidearm cast is necessary when a vertical cast would hit something overhead—tree branches or a bridge—or you need to cast around an object in front of you. Some casts, such as the roll and slack-line casts, combine a sidearm backcast with a vertical forward stroke.

The principles and timing of the sidearm delivery are the same as for an overhand delivery, but you can't make as long a cast with a sidearm delivery because the line is not as high off the water.

The starting position for the sidearm cast is much the same as the forward cast (page 35).

From the beginning of the backcast, however, the rod hand is held lower . . .

. . . bringing the rod back at an angle almost parallel to the water . . .

. . . and forward in the same plane.

Note how Lefty's elbow stays low through the entire sequence until the drop.

The roll cast is a forward cast without a backcast. It's so simple to learn that many instructors teach it before the forward cast. The roll cast is not as accurate as a regular forward cast and does not get as much distance. But it's necessary in a very common fishing situation: when your back is up against trees, brush, or anything that prevents you from making a normal backcast.

The key point to remember about a roll cast is that the form of the forward stroke is exactly the same as in a normal forward cast; only the setup is different.

To start, bring the rod back more slowly and farther than in a forward-cast pickup. Your goal is to get a portion of the line draping down behind the rod, while still leaving most of it in front of you on the water. Although the whole reason for doing a roll cast is that you have no room behind you for a backcast, the farther back you can bring your rod, the better.

The entire pickup for a roll cast should be slow and deliberate. Don't lift your rod so quickly that you pull too much line behind you. As in a forward cast, the point of the pickup is to get the line into position to load the rod. But here that load will be provided by the surface tension of the line lying on the water in front of you rather than the line straightening out in the air behind you.

Step 1. Pickup

With the line lying in front of you on the water, angle your rod slightly to the side, as in a sidearm cast. (If you hold it vertical, the line will hit the rod when you bring it back.) Lift the rod slowly, past the place you'd stop for a forward-cast pickup and as far back as you can without hitting any obstruction behind you. Remember to pivot your arm at the elbow and keep the elbow on the shelf. A common error in roll casting is thinking you have to lift your arm high to get the line off the water.

Casting

Step 2. Stop

Stop—just for an instant—before beginning the forward stroke. At this point, most of the line is still in front of you, but the rod tip should be back far enough that an arc of line is draping down slightly behind you. You must wait a split second for the line to stop moving rearward before beginning the forward stroke.

Use the same motion as in a normal forward cast: Bring the rod forward sharply, and stop it abruptly when line is shooting from the tip level with or at a slightly upward angle from the water. Although a roll-cast forward stroke is the same in form as a normal cast, it must be especially crisp because of the added force necessary to lift line off the water.

The drop is the same as in a forward cast, but it is especially important here to stop the rod dead and allow the forward-moving loop to unfurl in front of you before dropping the rod. After the line straightens in front of you over the water, let the rod drift down parallel to the water and allow the fly to settle.

The slack-line cast is a way to make the line land on the water in S-curves rather than a straight line. It is an essential technique for trout fishers because in many situations, if the line lands straight, the current catches it and pulls the fly downstream behind it, creating drag, an unnatural drift that instantly alerts trout that a fly is a counterfeit. If the line lands in curves, however, the current must first pull these out before it can pull the fly, and thus a slack-line cast allows the fly to drift some distance without drag.

The slack-line cast is most commonly used in two situations: when casting directly downstream or casting across-stream over a fast current lane into a slower one. Trout anglers routinely encounter these situations, and a slack-line cast is an essential in their repertoire.

Step 1. Backcast

Use the same basic form as in a forward cast. One tip: A sidearm backcast is easier to convert into the high-angle forward stroke you'll need for a slack-line cast.

Stop the rod sooner than you would for a normal forward stroke so the line shoots upward at a steep angle. Again remember Lefty's third principle: The line will go in the direction the rod tip is moving when it stops.

Casting

Step 3. Drop

The moment the line straightens in its upward path, drop the rod tip to the water. The forward part of the line will then fall to the surface in waves.

4

Trout Flies

You could fill a small library with books about trout flies and the insects they imitate. No subject in angling history has been so deeply studied, and any fly shop you enter will have bins and bins of flies in every shape, color, and size. Where do you start understanding this baffling array? This chapter provides a coherent overview of trout flies, a guide to the logic behind the patterns and what they imitate so you have a foundation upon which you can build however much knowledge you want. It also includes a selection of essential flies that will catch trout anywhere, so if you find entomology and fly-pattern details tedious, you can go right to the list of the basic dozen recommended flies at the end of the chapter and start fishing.

Above all, when choosing trout flies, current local information is irreplaceable. A pattern that works on one stream may not work on a neighboring stream, let alone on the other side of the country, and what works one day may not work the next. The patterns recommended in this chapter are ones that have proven successful over decades. They appear on the favorite-fly lists of experts all over the country, but each expert's list is slightly different, based on what has worked on his or her home water.

Trout flies can be divided into five basic types based on their construction and the food form they represent.

Dry Flies

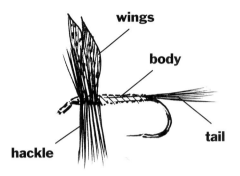

Dry flies imitate the adult stage of aquatic insects floating on the surface of the stream.

They stay afloat because of their architecture and buoyant construction materials. Most are tied with hackle—the stiff fibers from certain bird feathers—flared around the hook to imitate the insect's legs. The fly sits on the water on its hackle tips, keeping the body up off the surface. Flies without hackle are kept afloat with buoyant body and wing materials. The body of a dry fly is represented by natural or synthetic material, called dubbing, wound around the hook shaft. The wings are fashioned from feathers or hair, and the tails from natural or synthetic fibers.

If you set a fly next to the insect it imitates, you will immediately notice that the fly is a rough impression, not an exact replica. It fools the trout partly because its size, shape, and color suggest the insect. That part of the counterfeit is the fly tier's skill; the other part is the angler's skill in making the fly behave like the real thing.

Although a Hendrickson dry fly, which imitates the Ephemerella subvaria *species of mayfly, doesn't look much like the real thing when viewed side-by-side above water, its profile, size, hue, and "footprint" on the water are enough to fool the trout when viewed from below.*

Wet Flies

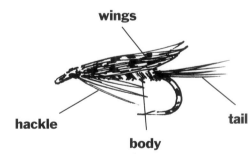

Wet flies imitate drowned adult insects or certain types of insects just before they emerge. They are designed to sink: They do not have stiff hackle wound around the hook, and the wings, cut from sections of feather, are folded back along the hook. Wet flies were actually the first type of fly ever devised, dating back to the 1600s in England, and once were standard in all fly boxes. They have since been largely replaced by nymphs as the underwater fly of choice.

Nymphs

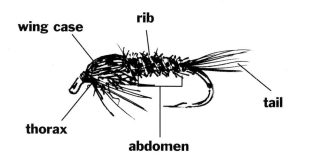

Nymphs imitate the underwater phase—nymph, larva, or pupa—of aquatic insects before they emerge as adults, and trout eat them all year long. Most nymphs are small and sparsely tied, a fuzzy body with no wings or hackle, and most are weighted to make them sink to the bottom, where natural nymphs and larvae live.

Terrestrials

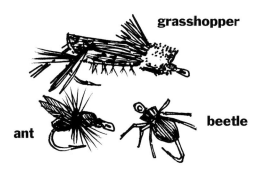

Terrestrials, sometimes grouped with dry flies because they float, imitate land-based insects including ants, beetles, and grasshoppers. Ant and beetle patterns are commonly made from molded foam and are very realistic. Most grasshopper patterns are made from traditional fly-tying materials, including deer hair and turkey feathers, and are more impressionistic.

Streamers

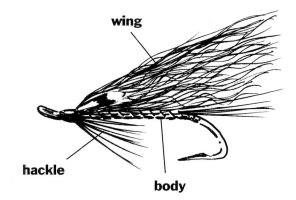

Streamers imitate baitfish. They are tied from long strands of natural or synthetic hair and fibers on long-shaft hooks.

57

The size of a fly is designated according to the size hook on which it is tied. A size 14 Adams, for example, is tied on a size 14 hook. The hook-sizing system is backward: The larger the number, the smaller the hook. Thus a size 30 hook is tiny, whereas a size 1 is huge. Most trout flies fall between sizes 12 and 18. Streamers and Woolly Buggers are generally large flies, sizes 4 through 12, and midges, which imitate a class of tiny aquatic insects, are tied all the way down to size 30, which is about the size of a comma on this page.

When trout are feeding selectively on a particular insect, matching the size of the fly to the size of the insect is the most crucial factor in selection. Many times the exact pattern in a size too large will be refused, whereas a pattern slightly off in color or design will catch fish if it is exactly the size of the insect the trout are feeding on or slightly smaller. When in doubt, always err on the small side.

Fly fishers also use hook size to express insect size. For example, they will observe a particular a hatch of mayflies and deem them a size 16. After handling flies for a season, you'll be able to gauge the size of a fly by glancing at it, and if you observe insects on the stream, you'll soon be able to estimate their size in the same terms.

The dramatic difference in size between a size 10 (bottom) and 16 of the same pattern (an Adams) illustrates the importance of choosing the size that matches the insects on the water. Trout will often refuse a fly that is even one size larger than the natural.

AQUATIC INSECTS

The vast majority of trout flies imitate aquatic insects, because that is the class of creatures that trout eat more than anything else. Naturally, then, fly-fishing for trout becomes more interesting and rewarding the more you learn about aquatic entomology. On the other hand, you don't need to know a thing about entomology to begin catching trout with some time-tested generic patterns. But whatever fly you tie on imitates something, and knowing what it is will help you catch fish.

You may recall dimly from biology class the seven categories into which scientists group living things: kingdom, phylum, class, order, family, genus, and species. Insecta is the class of most concern to trout fishers, and within that broad category, most flies are imitations of three orders. Mayflies (order Ephemeroptera) have historically been the most important aquatic insect to fly fishers, because their hatches are concentrated and highly visible. Caddisflies (order Trichoptera) are next in significance to anglers, followed by stoneflies (order Plecoptera). Trout eat other aquatic insects too, including dragonflies, damselflies, water bugs, and a variety of tiny species known generically as midges. They also eat terrestrial insects (ants, beetles, and grasshoppers), crustaceans (scuds, sow bugs, and crayfish), leeches, and baitfish. But the heart of fly fishing is fooling trout with aquatic insect imitations, and understanding the life cycles of mayflies, caddisflies, and stoneflies is the most logical place to begin building a working knowledge of trout flies.

Trout Flies

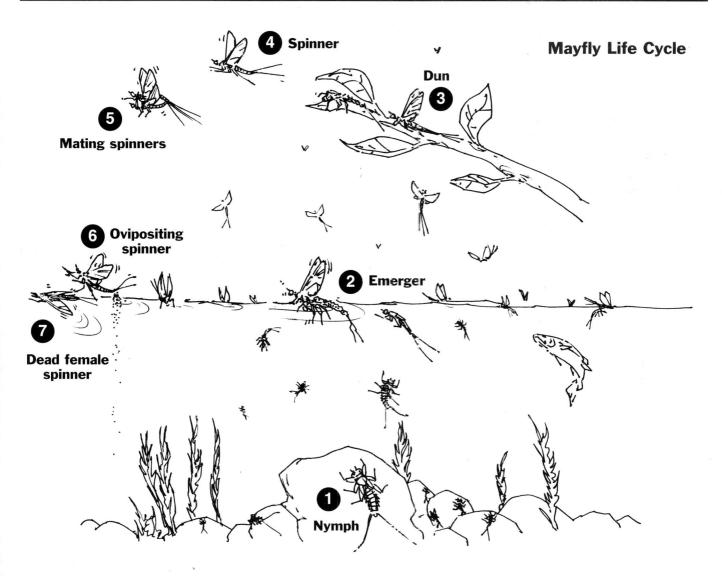

Mayfly Life Cycle

4 Spinner

3 Dun

5 Mating spinners

6 Ovipositing spinner

2 Emerger

7

Dead female spinner

1 Nymph

Mayfly nymphs hatch from eggs on the stream bottom and then live there for up to a year. When they are ready to become adults—most often during the spring or summer—they rise to the surface and struggle out of their nymphal skins, a brief process during which they are known as emergers. Once an emerger's wings are dry, it is known as a dun. The duns fly to streamside vegetation, where they molt a final time and become spinners, sexually mature adults. Male and female spinners mate in flight over the water, after which the female deposits her eggs (oviposits) by flying low and dipping her abdomen into the water. The spent female then dies and floats downstream.

Mayflies begin as eggs deposited on the water's surface by female mayfly adults, which die shortly thereafter. From the eggs come nymphs, which breathe with gills and live off algae on the stream bottom for up to a year. During this time, the nymphs molt several times, shedding their skins as their bodies expand and gradually develop into the winged adult.

When the adult form is fully developed within the nymph's case, the body floats to the surface. There on the surface, the case, called a nymphal shuck, splits, and the adult mayfly emerges onto the surface of the water. During the process of shedding its case, which may take seconds or minutes, the mayfly is known as an emerger. Once the mayfly is free of its case, it is known as a dun. Duns float along until their wings are dry and then fly to the branches of streamside bushes or trees, where they molt a final time and become spinners, the final and reproductive stage of their lives.

The entire mating cycle lasts only a day or two. First, the females are impregnated in a mating flight above the water. After mating, the females fly to streamside vegetation to let their eggs fertilize, then return to the stream to deposit them by dipping their abdomens to the surface. When the egg laying is over, the spent females plummet to the water in an event called a spinner fall. The male spinners, in contrast, typically die on the banks of the stream, caught in spiderwebs or eaten by other insects.

Adult mayfly. The most obvious feature of the mayfly dun is its pair of prominent, upright wings, which give the insect a sailboat profile on the water. Mayflies also have two or three long tails.

Trout eat mayflies in all their phases—nymph, emerger, dun, and spinner—and countless fly patterns have been created to imitate each phase. Considering the brevity of the adult's life, it would seem a disproportionate number of patterns are devoted to this phase, but once you experience the thrill of being on the water with the right fly during a big mayfly hatch, you'll appreciate why.

Mayfly and Generic Nymph Patterns

The first thing you need to know is that nymphs inhabit the stream all year long and trout feed on them continually. There is hardly a wrong time to fish a nymph. Second, because various species of nymphs in different stages of development are always present in the stream, trout aren't as choosy about them as they are about dry flies during a hatch, when the fish see a large number of identical adults in a brief period. Therefore, anglers can rely on a few generic nymph patterns to catch trout throughout the year.

Pheasant Tail nymph, beadhead version

The Pheasant Tail nymph imitates nymphs of the *Baetis* genus of mayfly, which includes the blue-winged olive, one of the most widespread mayflies on the continent. Thus the Pheasant Tail should be a staple in any fly box. *Baetis* nymphs are small, even for nymphs, so sizes 14, 16, and 18 are most useful.

The Prince nymph and Dave Whitlock's Squirrel nymph patterns are other generic nymphs that continue to produce in a variety of situations.

Prince nymph

Squirrel nymph

Gold-Ribbed Hare's Ear nymph

The Gold-Ribbed Hare's Ear is a generic pattern that catches fish everywhere simply because it resembles many underwater bugs, both mayfly nymphs and caddis larvae. Get several in sizes 12, 14, and 16.

Beadhead versions of the Gold-Ribbed Hare's Ear and Pheasant Tail have proven to be very effective variations of the basic pattern, and many anglers carry them exclusively.

Finally, some experts believe that trout take Woolly Buggers for large stonefly nymphs, yet another reason to carry this universally effective pattern.

Woolly Bugger

Mayfly Emerger Patterns

Mayflies are completely vulnerable to trout during the brief period when they first emerge and begin to shed their cases on the surface of the stream. The trout already know something's up, because they've been following the progress of the hatch, eating nymphs as they float to the surface. Now the emergers are floating by like sitting ducks, struggling out of their shucks, unable to fly.

Although the first, and for a long time the only, mayfly patterns imitated duns, ingenious tiers have since created emerger patterns by replacing traditional tail material with a tuft of synthetic yarn to represent the nymphal shuck being cast off. These patterns sometimes attract trout when dun patterns fail. If fish are rising to a hatch but ignoring your fly, try switching to the emerger version of the same fly. It often does the trick.

Sparkle Dun emerger

One of the most successful emerger patterns is the Sparkle Dun, which is tied in a number of colors, olive and tan being two of the most productive.

Mayfly Dun Patterns

More dry-fly patterns imitate mayfly duns than any other type or phase of insect. The dun appeals to the fly tier because it is the fully formed adult, with wings upright and body free of the nymphal shuck, and to the angler and entomologist because it is the most visible and dramatic stage of a hatch. Because dun patterns are such a broad category, it is useful to break them down further into three general designs.

CATSKILL DRY FLIES

Light Cahill

Hendrickson

This is the classic dry-fly design. These first American dry flies were created to float high on the fast riffles of the Catskill trout streams of New York State and thus evolved as a design with hackle wound 360 degrees around the hook. No matter how the fly lands on the water, it sits on its hackle tips, making it float high and stay visible in choppy water. Some Catskill patterns imitate particular mayfly species, especially those with large and regular hatches. The Hendrickson imitates the female *Ephemeralla subvaria*, a prolific and regular early-season mayfly on eastern streams. The Light Cahill is a more generic pattern that imitates a variety of light-colored eastern mayfly duns. The Blue-Winged Olive is also a generic pattern that represents duns of the *Baetis* genus, a small olive-hued mayfly found everywhere in America. Most mayfly duns occur in sizes 12 through 18. Check with your local fly shop or regional websites for size information before buying some.

Blue-Winged Olive

Adams

Royal Wulff

Even more generic yet are searching or attractor patterns, which imitate no particular insect at all. Two traditional styles that have proven remarkably productive over the years are the Adams and the Royal Wulff.

COMPARADUN AND PARACHUTE PATTERNS

The weakness of a traditional dry fly is that it sits unnaturally on the water, with its body propped up on its hackles rather than lying on the surface like a mayfly dun's. This discrepancy often makes no difference to the trout, especially if the surface of the water is broken and the fly is drifting quickly. But in water that is slow and clear enough for the trout to get a good look at a fly, alternative pattern styles often fool fish a Catskill fly will not.

Comparadun

The Comparadun, originated by Al Caucci and Bob Nastasi, is a simple, generic mayfly dun pattern tied in a variety of shades to approximate a number of species. Its significant design feature is that it has no hackle, and its deer-hair wings angle up and away from the body like a real mayfly's. Thus the fly's body sits on the

water, presenting a more realistic "footprint" when viewed from below by the trout. But because they have no hackle, Comparaduns don't float as high as traditional patterns and are harder to see as they drift. Also, their bodies tend to absorb water and must be kept dressed with floatant to maintain their buoyancy.

Parachute Adams

Traditional parachute patterns have a white wingpost, though in this variation, the Brite Wing Parachute Adams from Umpqua Feather Merchants, it is bright red. Either parachute pattern is more visible to the fisherman than the traditional Adams.

Parachute patterns are so-called because the hackle, instead of being wound around the hook shaft, is wound in a circular pattern around a wingpost on top of the shaft, allowing the fly's body to sit down on the water and present a more realistic footprint. Parachute patterns do gain some buoyancy from their hackle, however, so they ride slightly higher than patterns with no hackle at all. The Parachute Adams has become a standard in many fly boxes because it fools picky fish in situations where they might refuse a traditional Adams. Another advantage to the Parachute Adams is that its bright-colored wingpost (usually white, but also available in other bright colors) makes the fly much easier to follow on the water than the drab traditional pattern, especially when fishing riffles or in low light.

A general guideline for choosing between Catskill and alternative dun patterns is to use Catskill patterns in riffles or fast runs and alternative patterns, such as Comparaduns and parachutes, in pools, flats, and slower runs. The overriding principle in all fishing, however, is to use what works. If you're catching fish in a glassy pool with a Catskill fly, why change it? The point is that if your dry-fly box contains different styles, you'll have something to switch to when the fish aren't hitting.

Mayfly Spinner Patterns

When the mayfly dun sheds its skin the final time to become a spinner, it is brighter and more slender than before the molt, and its wings become transparent. When spinners fall to the water, they lie with their wings flat on the surface, perpendicular to their bodies, details that distinguish them immediately from duns. Because they lie so flat, spinners are much harder for the fisher to see than the duns with their upright wings, and many an angler has been perplexed by spinner falls, watching fish rise to invisible flies and then failing to catch any on dun imitations.

CDC Biot Spinner, pale morning dun

Spinner falls are relatively brief and typically occur in the evening. Though the window of opportunity for fishing them is smaller than for fishing duns, trout feast on spinners eagerly, and if you are lucky enough to be on the water during a spinner fall, you'll hope you have some spinner patterns in your box. The Rusty Spinner and Pale Morning Dun Spinner are good generic patterns that cover two of the most common colors.

Rusty Spinner

Caddisfly Life Cycle

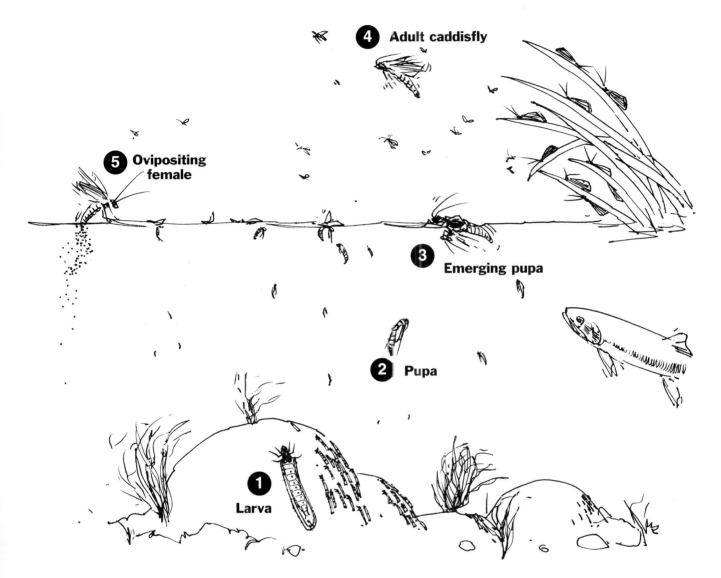

4 Adult caddisfly

5 Ovipositing female

3 Emerging pupa

2 Pupa

1 Larva

Caddisfly eggs hatch on the stream bottom and live there as grublike larvae for most of the year. A few weeks before becoming adults, they transform into pupae and float to the surface, where the pupal skin splits and they fly off. Adults mate in flight above the stream, after which the female deposits her eggs.

Although mayflies were long the primary focus of fly tiers and fishers, we have since learned that in many streams, at many times of the year, caddisflies are even more important to the trout. Caddisflies don't get as much attention from us simply because their hatches are not as concentrated, visible, and dramatic as those of mayflies, and also, perhaps, because the bug isn't quite as photogenic. Caddisflies look like moths. When

at rest, their wings fold over their bodies like little tents, making them instantly distinguishable from mayflies, whose prominent wings stand upright when the insect is at rest.

The caddisfly's one-year life cycle is similar to that of the mayfly but differs in a few details important to fly fishers. Like mayflies, caddisflies begin as eggs deposited in the water by adult females, but they go

Trout Flies

through two aquatic forms, larva and pupa, before emerging as adults. The grublike larvae live on the stream bottom for most of the year, and most species build a case around themselves from available materials, including tiny sticks and pebbles. Other caddis larvae are free-swimming. Whatever its larval form, a week or two before hatching into an adult, the caddis larva enters the pupal stage by spinning a cocoon around itself, within which the winged adult develops. When the adult is fully formed, it cuts its way out of the pupal case, rises to the surface, and flies off. Although some caddis pupae drift for quite a ways before emerging, they generally do not struggle once they arrive on top, like mayfly emergers, nor do they float along drying their wings. Caddisflies just pop out and take off. The adults live up to a month and are often seen flying in swarms upstream to mate.

Adult caddisfly. These insects carry their wings folded against the body like a pup tent. They resemble moths.

Caddisfly hatches are not the surface carnivals that mayfly hatches can be, for either the trout or the trout fisher. Caddis pupae hatch sporadically throughout the season rather than in large numbers at one time, as mayflies do. But trout eat plenty of caddisflies in all their phases, and you should carry a few patterns in your box.

Caddis Larva Patterns

Green Caddis Larva

Zug Bug

Most caddis larvae patterns imitate free-swimming caddis rather than case builders. A Green Caddis Larva and Tan Caddis Larva pattern in sizes 12 and 14 are good imitations. Many anglers also use a Zug Bug, a generic nymph pattern that catches a lot of trout in many situations, when fish are feeding on caddis larvae.

Caddis Pupa Patterns

Nemes Soft-Hackle

Sparkle Pupa

Trout eat caddis pupae eagerly, partly because they are much more accessible than the larvae, especially after the pupae begin drift toward the surface to emerge. The Partridge and Yellow and Sylvester Nemes's Soft-Hackle patterns are generic wet flies that work well during pupae hatches. Gary LaFontaine's Sparkle Pupa is a more recent and imitative pattern.

Caddis Dry-Fly Patterns

Elk Hair Caddis

Caddis adults are drab insects with fewer variations in color and form than mayflies, so a few generic patterns will suffice. One of the most reliable is the Elk Hair Caddis, sometimes called the Elk Wing Caddis. If you poll veteran fly fishers on the essential dry flies to carry, the Elk Hair Caddis will likely appear on every list.

The Henryville Special is a caddis adult imitation in the quill-wing style (in this case, mallard-feather sections), which creates a more realistic profile, useful in fooling trout in smooth water.

Henryville Special

Stonefly Life Cycle

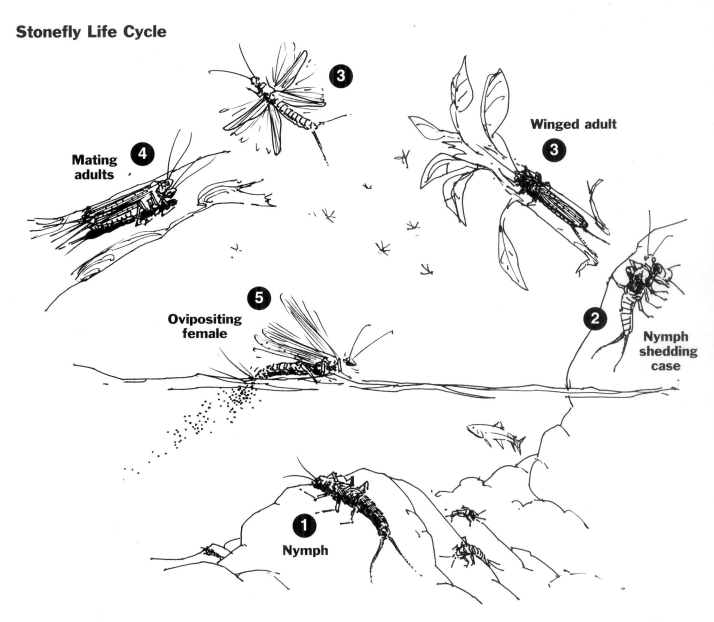

Mating adults 4

3

Winged adult 3

Nymph shedding case 2

Ovipositing female 5

Nymph 1

Stonefly nymphs can live underwater from one year in smaller species to as long as four years in the larger species. Unlike mayflies and caddisflies, the nymphs do not float to the surface but crawl out on shore, where they shed their nymphal skins and become winged adults. The adults mate on rocks or vegetation, after which the female deposits her eggs.

Stoneflies are not available to trout in as many forms or at as many times of the season as mayflies and caddisflies and thus are not as widely represented in fly patterns. They are found all over the country, however, and trout sometimes feed on them selectively, so it makes sense to carry a few patterns.

Nymphs are commonly found in runs and riffles with rocky bottoms. They need oxygen-rich water, which means fast or cold water, so they tend to inhabit freestone streams in northern latitudes, though they can tolerate slow water if it stays cold year-round, as do some mountain lakes and western spring creeks.

These insects are generally less accessible to trout than mayflies and caddisflies. The nymphs live under and between rocks, where they're hard to get at, and the adults are not as aerial as mayflies and caddisflies, preferring to crawl around on streamside vegetation.

Trout Flies

Adult stonefly. Stoneflies are distinguished by long, flat wings held against the body when at rest. They are often seen on streamside rocks.

Stimulator

When stonefly nymphs are ready to emerge, they crawl along the bottom to shore. Once there, the nymphs shed their cases, and the adult stoneflies climb into streamside grasses, bushes, or trees, where they mate. The females deposit their eggs by flying low to the stream and dipping their abdomens onto the surface.

Stoneflies are most vulnerable to trout at two times: when the nymphs migrate to shore and when the females are depositing their eggs.

Yellow Stonefly dry fly

Golden Stone dry fly

Two species of giant stoneflies, the golden stone and the salmon fly, are famous on western rivers. When the 3-inch salmon flies are on the water in Montana, trout hit them with abandon. The Montana Stone and Golden Stone are good patterns for giant stonefly nymphs, and the Improved Sofa Pillow and Stimulator for giant stonefly adults.

Most stoneflies are much smaller. Yellow Stonefly dry is a good choice to imitate the widespread yellow sally stonefly, which occurs all over the country and hatches in midsummer. The Gold-Ribbed Hare's Ear can be used to imitate the nymph.

Improved Sofa Pillow

Muddler Minnow

Matuka

Marabou Muddler

Zonker

Black-Nosed Dace

Hornberg

Mickey Finn

Streamers imitate small baitfish, and though they do not catch anywhere near the number of trout that insect imitations do, they account for some of the largest. The reason is simple: Big trout look for big meals, and a baitfish has a lot more calories than an insect. Perhaps the most productive streamer of all time is the Muddler Minnow, which imitates the ubiquitous sculpin, a bottom-dwelling baitfish. The Marabou Muddler variation adds the appeal of undulating marabou feathers. Other popular patterns are the Black-Nose Dace, Zonker, Hornberg, Mickey Finn, and Matuka (originally from New Zealand).

Trout Flies

Terrestrials

Dave's Hopper

Attractor Ant

Foam Beetle

Ants, beetles, and grasshoppers are eagerly eaten by trout, especially during the summer months on meadow streams where they fall or are blown into the water from streamside grasses or bushes. Dave's Hopper, created by Dave Whitlock, is a very successful grasshopper imitation and catches some big fish. You should also carry a Black Ant and a Foam Beetle.

Woolly Bugger

Woolly Bugger

The Woolly Bugger is in its own category because no one is certain whether trout take it for a baitfish, nymph, leech, or crayfish. Russell Blessing of Lancaster, Pennsylvania, invented the pattern in 1967, when he tied a marabou tail onto a Woolly Worm in an attempt to imitate a hellgrammite. Whatever it imitates, the trout continue to hit it, and you should have several sizes in olive and black in your box. You may also want to try the many varieties with beadheads and flashy body and tail material.

Gold Bead Woolly Bugger

Gold Bead Crystal Bugger

Identifying Aquatic Insects

Most fly fishers eventually become entomologists at some level. The first level is simply learning to recognize the most common hatches (emergences of adult insects) on your home water and knowing the patterns that imitate them. The second level is collecting specimens from the stream and inspecting them more closely. The third level is bringing these specimens home and tying flies that imitate them exactly. But you don't have to be any level of entomologist to notice that insects are emerging and try to match them. Here is one approach to begin identifying insects.

First, get a field guide to aquatic insects. Three good ones are *An Angler's Guide to Aquatic Insects and Their Imitations,* by Rick Hafele and Scott Roederer; *Instant Mayfly Identification Guide,* by Al Caucci and Bob Nastasi; and *Handbook of Hatches,* by Dave Hughes. If you want to catch some insects to inspect them more closely, buy an aquarium net and carry it in your vest or pack. If you want to bring the insects home, take along a small vial or jar.

Then find a website or guidebook that lists the starting and ending dates of the significant hatches on your home water, and buy some flies that match these insects.

Armed with some fly patterns and your field guide, get out on the stream. Keep in mind that most hatches start in the afternoon, when the water warms up. The most obvious clue that a hatch is on is fish rising repeatedly in a particular stretch of water. It can be hard to figure out what they're rising to. Once you see the rise, the insect is gone. Also, rising trout are often feeding on tiny insects, too small to see, or on subsurface nymphs just before they emerge. If you're lucky, you may be able to follow a floating insect and see it disappear in a swirl. Then again, if the hatch is prolific, there may be enough insects and rises for you to deduce what the trout are eating without witnessing an actual take.

Next, try to catch one of the insects and identify it. Even if you don't have a field guide, note the insect's size and color and see if you have a fly that matches it. The acid test is whether the fish think so, which you'll find out when you tie it on. Few situations in fishing are as exciting as being on the water during a big hatch with the right dry fly.

Fishing with Searching Patterns

Like all successful predators, trout are opportunists that in most situations will eat anything that looks edible, and a handful of generic flies—patterns that don't imitate any particular species—keep on catching fish. The Woolly Bugger, Adams, Royal Wulff, Elk Hair Caddis, and Gold-Ribbed Hare's Ear nymph are hall-of-fame searching patterns that every angler, beginner or veteran, should carry. If trout are not feeding selectively, which on many streams is most of the time, these patterns and others like them will almost always catch fish.

A Basic Fly Box

Admittedly, trout flies and aquatic entomology are daunting subjects, especially to those not inclined to details and science. Some fly fishers become captivated by entomology, and others become totally absorbed by the craft of fly tying. But many others try fly fishing simply because they are drawn to fly casting and catching fish on a fly and are satisfied to read hatch charts and buy flies ready-made. Whatever your preference, don't be intimidated by the complexity of fly patterns. You don't need to know a thing about bugs or the theory of fly design to start catching fish and having fun.

The following collection of flies will catch trout anywhere in the world. Each pattern is followed by recommended sizes to carry.

The Basic Dozen

NYMPHS
Gold-Ribbed Hare's Ear (12, 14, 16)
Pheasant Tail (14, 16, 18)

DRY FLIES
Adams (14, 16)
Parachute Adams (14, 16)
Royal Wulff (12, 14)
Elk Hair Caddis (12, 14, 16)
Blue-Winged Olive (14, 16, 18)
PMD Comparadun (14, 16, 18)
Sparkle Dun (14, 16, 18)

STREAMERS
Muddler Minnow (8, 10)

WOOLLY BUGGERS
Olive Woolly Bugger (8, 10)
Black Woolly Bugger (8, 10)

5

Trout Fishing

5

Trout Fishing

Be warned: Fly-fishing for trout can easily become a lifetime pursuit. A good part of the appeal is that both the fish and the waters they inhabit are beautiful. Trout can't tolerate warm or polluted water, and fly fishers as a group tend to be nature-loving, conservation-minded people, the type who pick up litter along the stream and return the fish they catch unharmed. As a result, trout streams are often the nicest water you'll ever see. Add to this the appeal of fly casting, fly tying, and amateur entomology, and you have a sport that can absorb you for the rest of your life.

B rown, rainbow, and brook are the three species of trout the American angler is most likely to encounter. Brown and rainbow trout are by far the most widespread species in North America and have been widely stocked all over the United States. Brook trout are native to the northeastern United States and Canada but have also been stocked throughout the country. Cutthroat trout are native to the West, though their numbers have declined in recent decades as a result of habitat degradation.

Brown Trout

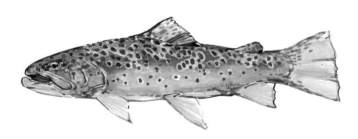

Introduced to America from Europe in the 1880s, the brown trout has become a favorite of American fly fishers. It can tolerate slightly warmer water than other trout and therefore has been most widely stocked. It can grow to 8 or 9 pounds in some waters and has the reputation of being harder to fool than other species. Large browns that have been in the stream for several seasons are real prizes.

Rainbow Trout

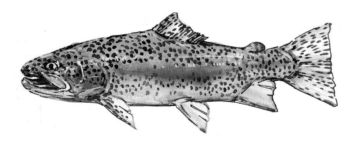

Native to the western United States, rainbows are colorful fish with the reputation of being jumpers and fighters. Given the opportunity, they migrate downstream to the ocean. In the West, they return to their home rivers to spawn, at which point they take on a silvery hue and are known as steelheads. Rainbows are now widely stocked all over the country.

Brook Trout

Native to the eastern United States and Canada (hence, the nickname "native"), wild brook trout still inhabit remote waters in the Northeast, where they are a treasured resource. Brook trout hit flies and lures eagerly and so can be easily depleted from heavily fished waters. Those in small mountain ponds and streams tend to be small and numerous, whereas the sea-run brook trout of Canada's maritime provinces can reach 10 pounds.

Cutthroat Trout

Named for the two red streaks below the jaw, cutthroats are native to the West Coast and the Rocky Mountains. They are less tolerant of pollution than other species and more susceptible to fishing pressure and thus are carefully protected in streams where they still thrive.

The first thing you should do with your fly rod when you approach a trout stream is . . . nothing. Don't get in the water, don't begin casting. Instead, spend the first ten or fifteen minutes scouting the water. Put on your polarized sunglasses, slow down, and look.

The goal of this section is to help you avoid one of the most common causes of failure on the trout stream: fishing where there are no fish. Learning to read a trout stream is fun and relatively easy. You don't need electronic equipment and hydrographic charts, as you do to find fish in a deep lake. The current in a trout stream makes its features obvious, and because the water is relatively shallow and clear, you can often see the fish.

Stream Anatomy

The fishable water in most trout streams comprises four water types: riffles, runs, pools, and flats. Recognizing these water types and how trout behave in them will help you find and catch fish.

Riffles. A riffle is a stretch of fast, relatively shallow water, with a broken surface created by water flowing over a bottom covered with small or medium-size rocks. Riffles are not as turbulent as rapids or falls but have choppier surfaces than runs. They are rich in insect life, because the stony bottom provides cracks and crevices for nymphs and larvae, but the relatively shallow and fast water of riffles is less-than-ideal trout holding water. As a rule, bigger fish prefer the deeper, slower water of runs and pools, where they don't have to fight the current and can dive into deep holes when threatened. On the other hand, the trout in riffles tend to be less skittish than those in pools, because the choppy surface makes them less visible to predators from above, and the noise of the fast water helps disguise your footsteps as you wade. Trout in riffles are also less selective about fly patterns. For one thing, the broken surface obscures their view of the fly, and for another, the fast current carries it by them quickly, so they tend to make quick decisions. Contrast this to the situation in a pool or flat, where the trout have ample time to inspect a pattern that is moving slowly or not at all on a glassy surface.

Riffles are characterized by fast water and a choppy surface. Most riffles are best fished with underwater flies, especially nymphs. Slower riffles can be fished with high-riding dry flies, such as Catskill or Wulff patterns, whereas sparsely-tied dry flies are quickly dragged under.

The surface of a run or glide is less choppy than a riffle, but the water is moving faster than that in a pool. Runs can be fished with any type of fly, wet or dry, and often hold many fish.

A flat is a level, shallow area, usually on the inside bend of a river. This is the famous Railroad Ranch section of the Henry's Fork in Idaho. Fish sometimes move into flats to feed on insect hatches, but the still, shallow water makes them skittish and they must be approached carefully. Keep low, and don't get too close.

Pools are relatively deep areas where the bottom of the stream is bowl-shaped or level, producing a slow current and calm surface. The angler here is standing at the bottom or tail of the pool and casting upstream toward its head. Because of the unbroken surface and high visibility within this kind of water, fish in pools tend to be wary.

Runs. A run has a noticeable current but a smoother surface than a riffle because the water is a bit deeper and the gradient of the streambed not quite as steep. A run usually has rocks scattered along its length, but these produce swirls and boils on the surface rather than the even chop of a riffle.

Runs almost always hold trout because they provide all their needs: relatively deep water to afford some protection from predators and enough current to bring a steady drift of insects, yet not so swift that the trout has to expend too much energy fighting it. The runs that are most appealing to trout have good-size rocks, chutes, or eddies as holding places. Fishing a run requires more water-reading skill than fishing riffles or pools, simply because a run has more features. It also requires some casting skill to present your fly naturally, without drag.

Pools. A pool is a stretch of deep water where the current is slow, sometimes barely perceptible. The bottom is usually bowl-shaped. A pool in a small trout stream may be as short as 10 feet, whereas one in a big river can be a mile long. At the head or top of the pool, where the water enters, there is usually a row of rocks or a ledge across the stream, with water pouring down into the pool in chutes. After that, the pool widens into its body before narrowing again at the tail, where the water speeds up as it descends into the next riffle or run. Pools are often home to the largest trout in the stream, because their depth offers the most protection from predators and their stillwater requires the least energy from the trout to maintain their positions. Also, the water at the bottom of a pool will stay cooler and more oxygenated than the upper layer in the heat of summer.

Trout are not always as evenly distributed in a pool as in a run, however, because there are fewer prime feeding stations where the current brings food past their noses. Also, the flat surface of a pool makes trout wary. They tend to stay down and out of sight, so fishing a pool requires more stealth than fishing runs or riffles.

Flats. Flats are shallow, level-bottomed areas of streams, often on the inside of bends on larger streams and rivers. They are sometimes only inches deep and have little or no current. Trout sometimes move into flats in numbers to feed on insect hatches, but they are always very nervous there because the shallow water and glassy surface provide little protection. So though they sometimes offer great fishing opportunities, flats are a challenge to your trout-stalking and fly-presentation skills.

Trout Holding Places

Trout look for holding places that will provide three things: access to food, protection from predators, and the ability to do both with the least amount of energy and risk. Additionally, trout need more oxygen than warm-water species, so during prolonged hot spells, they tend to migrate into deeper or faster water, which contains more oxygen than slower or warmer water. Combine this knowledge of habitat with the fact that trout feed mainly on aquatic insects, and you begin to understand the significance of current in trout fishing. Insects are ruled by the current, whether as nymphs or larvae on the stream bottom or as adults floating on the surface. Trout spend most of every day hanging in the current, pointed upstream, waiting for insects.

A good place for a trout to lie is one where the current brings insects past its nose but does not require it to spend all its energy fighting the current. In a stream of constant depth and moderate current from bank to bank, trout may be anywhere. But most streams and rivers have differing depths, current speeds, and distributions of rocks in any given stretch, so certain places will hold trout and others will not. You will be much, much more successful if you concentrate your fishing on the spots that are likely to hold trout rather than covering every square inch of the stream and thus spending a good portion of your time casting to fishless water.

One of the most reliable guidelines for finding trout is to look for places where fast water meets slow: the edges of channels, behind rocks or other obstacles, the heads and tails of pools. The trout will be in the slower water, watching what the current is bringing them.

Current Edges. Trout like to hang on the edges of a fast current, where the water is slower but they're still very close to insects being swept downstream. Off to one side of a chute flowing between two rocks at the head of a pool and the edge of a channel in a run are likely holding places. Either situation fulfills the two criteria mentioned above: The current is a cafeteria line of insects, and being on the edge of it, in the slower water, allows the trout to wait where it doesn't have to fight the current.

Rocks. The pocket of water just behind, or downstream of, a rock is a classic trout holding place. The rock breaks the current, creating a little haven behind it, and the faster water rushing around each side sweeps insects right past the trout's nose. But a rock also interrupts the current in front and to the sides of it, so trout station themselves in these positions as well. The rock can range from the size of a toaster to that of a Volkswagen and may be partially or wholly submerged. In deep runs or pools, you may not be able to see the rock itself, only the swirl or boil on the surface. But wherever you find rocks in the current, you will find trout around them.

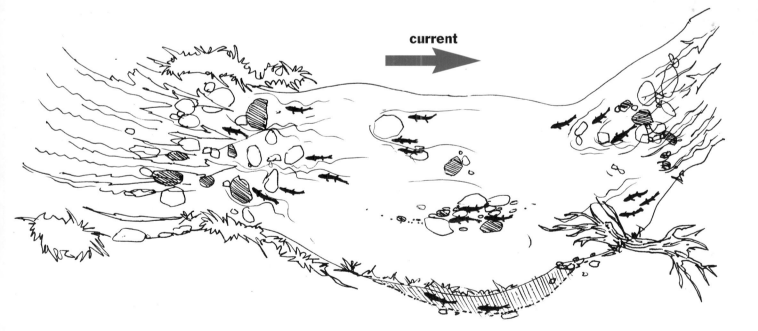

current

Trout Lies

Trout face upstream, waiting for food to drift down to them, and prefer spots behind rocks, fallen logs, or any object that breaks the current. They also tend to congregate at the head (at left) and tail (right) of a pool or run.

Submerged Tree Limbs. Like rocks, downed tree limbs break the current and make good trout lies.

Undercut Banks. Trout often hold in the curve on the outside of a stream bend where the current has cut into the bank and produced a little shelf over the water.

Heads and Tails of Pools. Trout may be anywhere in a pool, but they are likely to be concentrated at the head and tail, places where the water speeds up and funnels food into lanes. Heads of pool are particularly appealing, because this is where insects first arrive into the pool from the riffle or run above it. Trout will be stationed along the edges of the chutes bringing water into the pool or behind the ledge that marks the upper end of the pool. At the tail of a pool, the water again speeds

up as it narrows and drops into the next riffle or run. Trout often hang here as well, watching for insects before they are swept out of the pool.

Stalking Trout

Most of a trout's life is spent facing upstream, the direction from which food arrives. This observation leads to the first general rule of trout stalking: Whether walking along the bank or wading in the stream, you can approach a trout more closely when working upstream, because you're coming at the fish from behind. Some stretches can be approached only by wading downstream, however, and many fishers prefer to work in this direction simply because it's easier to wade with

Kneeling keeps you below the sight line of nearby fish, a tactic especially useful when approaching wary trout in small, clear streams.

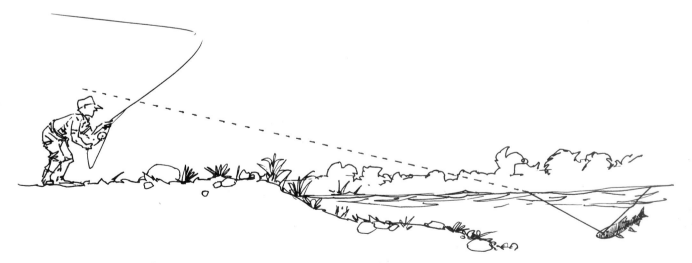

A trout's window of vision above the surface is increased by the refraction of light as it enters the water. However, the lower and farther away the object, the more likely it will fall outside the trout's window. Thus, the closer you approach, the more you need to lower your profile by stooping or kneeling in order to remain undetected.

the current than against it. Many anglers also prefer to cast dry flies downstream to a fish so that the fish sees the fly before the leader. Just remember that when you work downstream, you're moving toward fish that are looking in your direction.

The second rule in approaching trout is to stay low. Trout are extremely wary of danger from above, an instinct bred into them by millennia of escape from fish-eating birds. They will bolt at the first sight of movement above. Because light rays are bent when they enter the water, however, a trout's window of vision extends upward at an angle from its vantage point underwater such that it cannot see low-lying objects that are any distance away. Thus the farther away you are from a fish, the taller you can stand and not be detected, whereas the closer you get, the lower you have to be. One advantage to wading in the water rather than walking on the bank is that a good part of you is already below the surface. But when wading in shallow water or approaching trout closely, hunching down to lower your profile will decrease your chances of spooking them. When stalking trout from the bank, stay back from the edge of the stream; if you have to get closer, stay low. Some veterans get down on their hands and knees to scout a pool.

The third rule of stalking trout is to walk softly and slowly, especially when wading. Although trout do not hear, per se, they do sense vibrations acutely. Stomping on the bank or a wooden bridge above a stream will send them scattering for cover, and even a slight disturbance underwater will have the same effect, because vibrations travel so fast in water. If you wade carelessly or fast, kicking rocks or sending ripples across the surface, you'll scare every trout in the neighborhood. Underwater disturbances are especially noticeable in stillwater, so if you're fishing a quiet pool, wade in slow motion, lifting and placing one foot at a time. It also helps to wade with your body sideways or at an angle to the current, especially when going upstream; if you walk directly facing the current, you present a broader front and create more of a wake.

Finally, don't wade where you should be fishing. Scan the water before you step into it. Veteran guides shake their heads in frustration at the number of fishers who walk right over good trout water on their way somewhere else.

Spotting Trout

Seeing trout underwater requires some patience and some idea of where to look. But once you spot a few fish, it becomes easier. You get a knack for distinguishing fish from rocks or shadows on the bottom. A pool or run with clear water is a good place to start. Find a vantage point downstream of likely trout holding water,

Riseforms are easy to spot and may even hold clues as to what insect the fish are rising to. For example, trout often slash aggressively at caddisflies, which pop off the surface in a hatch, whereas they just sip dying mayfly spinners casually. Whenever you see a rise, keep your eye on that spot. If the fish is rising regularly, try to gauge its feeding rhythm and time your cast to the next rise.

put on your polarized glasses, stay low or back from the bank, and watch.

The most obvious giveaway that trout are in the area are riseforms, dimples made by fish taking surface insects. Though riseforms are easy to observe, the fish that make them may not be, because trout take insects in a flash and then sink back to their holding areas. If you see a riseform, watch that spot for a while. A trout tends to remain stationed beneath a particular current lane waiting for insects, and if you see one riseform, you will likely see another in the same place soon after, especially if insects are hatching. If you can't see the fish itself, adjust your sight line, stooping down or moving slowly to one side, until you can. Watching how trout feed will be instructive when you start dry-fly fishing.

If no fish are rising, find a fishy-looking stretch of water where you can see the bottom, or at least a few

Crushing Hook Barbs

Using barbless hooks is the key to releasing fish unharmed. A barb's only function is to prevent the hook from sliding out the hole it went in, so removing a barbed hook always involves some tearing of flesh or, if the fish is hooked deeply or in the gills, fatal injury. What's more, removing a barbed hook often requires lifting a fish out of the water and holding it tightly while working the barb free. A barbless hook, on the other hand, can be quickly removed with a little shake or a slight push in the direction opposite to which it entered, so a fish can often be released without even lifting it from the water.

Using barbless hooks has become standard practice among trout fly fishers, yet most commercial flies are still tied on barbed hooks. To eliminate the barb, simply squeeze it down to the hook shaft with a pair of pliers. In most cases, the barb will break off; if not, it will still be flattened against the shaft and rendered harmless.

An added bonus to using barbless hooks is the ease with which they can be removed from your own flesh, a feature beginning casters may come to appreciate on windy days.

To crush the barb of a hook, hold the pliers lengthwise along the hook shank and squeeze.

feet beneath the surface, and stand there for several minutes, just scanning the water. The key to spotting trout underwater is detecting movement. You may see something you thought was a rock move suddenly upstream a few feet. Or something you thought was a fish may turn out to be a strand of weeds waving on an underwater snag. Trout will hang in the same spot for several minutes, barely undulating in the current. But they do reposition themselves often—not moving far, but far enough for you to pick up the movement and make out the fish.

Sight-fishing for trout is great sport, and many guides do nothing else, fishing only to trout they can spot.

Walking slowly along the stream with polarized glasses, studying the water, is time wisely spent. Once you spot a few trout, you'll know what to look for, and an invisible world will gradually be revealed.

Most of a trout's diet consists of insects in their underwater phases. Although dry-fly fishing may be more dramatic, over the long run, fishing with nymphs, streamers, and wet flies is more productive. Also, because underwater flies require less casting finesse than dry flies, they are a good choice to begin learning the sport.

Fishing the Woolly Bugger

In *Essential Trout Flies*, Dave Hughes proclaims, "If I arrive at a piece of water I've never fished, nearly anywhere in the world, and am in doubt about what to use, I usually begin with an olive Woolly Bugger and try a black one next." That's a strong statement, especially from an author who has written more than twenty books on fly fishing, including the definitive *Trout Flies*, which covers some five hundred patterns.

Tackle for Woolly Buggers. Woolly Buggers are large, fluffy flies usually tied with lead wire around the shank to make them sink and often a beadhead to give them a jigging action. The combination of weight and wind resistance makes them unwieldy to cast with lightweight outfits and long, delicate leaders. Outfits of 5-weight and up are best; if your only rod is a 4-weight, you'll find Woolly Buggers in the smaller sizes (10 and 12) easier to cast. A 3X leader is about right for size 10 or 12 Woolly Buggers, but for sizes 8 and larger, a 2X will give you more control. In general, long leaders (9 feet and up) are not necessary to fool trout with underwater flies, and you may find casting a heavy fly easier with a 7 1/2-foot leader.

Woolly Bugger Tactics. To start fishing a stream with Woolly Buggers, find a riffle or run at least 2 feet deep and identify the most likely holding places within it. Picture the trout in these spots, facing upstream. When fishing this fly, the key thing to remember is that all the foods it imitates—leeches, sculpins, large nymphs—are found on the stream bottom, so that's where you want the fly to be.

Cast across and slightly upstream to a point that will let the fly drift by each likely holding place. Keep in mind that the stronger the current, the higher off the bottom it will carry any drifting object, including your fly, whereas the slower the current, the more quickly it will let drifting objects sink. Thus it's better to angle your cast more upstream in swift current, so you get a longer drift and the fly has more time to sink. When faced with a very swift, deep current or a situation

Woolly Bugger

where you have no choice but to cast downstream to reach the fish, you may have to add split shot to your leader or switch to a sinking-tip line. In any case, you have to get a Woolly Bugger down to the fish.

If you get no hit through a complete drift, retrieve the fly 10 or 15 feet back toward you by making short tugs with your line hand, pulling it between the thumb and forefinger of your rod hand. This retrieve is meant to make the fly imitate a leech, large nymph, or sculpin swimming upstream, and it sometimes triggers an aggressive strike.

Woolly Bugger Pattern Selection. Since the Woolly Bugger is not meant to imitate a specific insect or minnow, you need not be too picky about pattern details, but here are some general guidelines. The first consideration, as always, is size, but because the trout won't be comparing this imitation to a hatch of insects, a range of sizes will work. Woolly Buggers are commonly tied in sizes 6 through 12, with 8 and 10 the most popular. Choose the size that is easiest to cast with your outfit.

About color, take Dave Hughes's advice: An olive Woolly Bugger is an excellent first choice for prospecting most waters, with black second. Another useful generalization is that olive is better for clearer water, whereas black is more visible in murkier water. Many anglers choose black for early-season fishing when the water is discolored.

You'll see many variations of the basic pattern in catalogs and fly shops, including flies with strands of flashy material in the tail and wild colors such as hot pink and lime in the body. You will also find beadhead versions. When considering variations, keep in mind that local fly shops tend to carry those that work in nearby streams. Check the bins for a particular pattern that seems to sell in quantity and give it a try.

Fishing with Nymphs

To a trout fisher, *nymph* is a generic term for the immature stages of several aquatic insects, including caddisfly larvae and pupae and mayfly nymphs. Experienced trout fishers devote a lot of time to nymphs simply because trout devote a lot of time to them. In fact, nymphs constitute the biggest part of most trout's diets.

Tackle for Nymphs. With the exception of large stonefly nymphs, most nymph patterns for trout are small, between sizes 12 and 16, and compact, with little wind resistance. These factors, along with the fact that trout take nymphs with the most inconspicuous of hits—they just inhale them—recommend light tackle for nymph fishing. One caveat: Like Woolly Buggers, nymphs are fished on the bottom, so their hooks are of heavier gauge than dry-fly hooks and are often wrapped with lead wire for additional weight. Also, beadhead nymphs have become very popular, and the bead adds weight. So though nymphs are small and aerodynamic, they are often heavier than they appear—much heavier than the same size dry fly—and weighted versions may be cumbersome to cast with outfits under 4-weight.

Nymph Tactics. When starting out nymph fishing, look for a riffle or run with a constant current all the way across. If possible, avoid wide runs with complex current patterns, because it's tricky to get a natural drift in such water. Also avoid still, clear pools, which are challenging environments in which to fool trout.

Nymphs are fished much like Woolly Buggers: You cast them up- or across-stream and let them drift down along the bottom. Most nymphs are small critters, at the mercy of the current. They drift downstream almost continually in a trout stream, and trout hang there, facing upstream, waiting to intercept them. Though trout seldom demand an exact nymph imitation, they'll ignore as inedible something floating unnaturally. The fly fisher's enemy here is drag.

Nymph Pattern Selection. At certain times, gangs of nymphs emerge to the surface at once, an event that triggers selective feeding by trout and may require you to duplicate the insect du jour very closely. But most times, trout feed opportunistically on whatever nymphs the current brings them, and you can fool them with

A well-stocked nymph box.

A strike indicator, placed on the leader a distance from the fly that is at least twice the depth of the water, acts like a tiny bobber, telegraphing even the most delicate strike.

something that looks roughly like something they've eaten before.

A few generic nymph patterns will catch lots of fish everywhere, and you need not go any further unless you want to specialize in nymphing. Start with some Gold-Ribbed Hare's Ears in sizes 12, 14, and 16 and Pheasant Tail nymphs in sizes 14 and 16. Buy several in each size, because if you're fishing them correctly, they bump the bottom and tend to snap off on snags.

Detecting Strikes with Nymphs. The trickiest part of nymph fishing is detecting a strike. Trout strikes on nymphs are subtle. Actually, *strike* is far too strong a word for the way trout inhale these small insects. The signal of a pickup is difficult to feel, easier to see. It's most often just a slight upstream twitch of the line as the fly drifts downstream, and sometimes only a hesitation. The effect on your end is not much different from the nymph bumping something on the bottom, but you never know. When in doubt, set the hook.

Some anglers simply watch the line where it enters the water for a twitch (another reason to use brightly colored line), but strike indicators, which act as tiny bobbers, make pickups much more visible. As a rule of thumb, attach the strike indicator to your leader a distance from your nymph that is twice the depth of the water. Thus if the water is 2 feet deep, attach the indicator 4 feet from your nymph. This distance allows the nymph to get down to the bottom on a drift. If the water is very slow, you can shorten the distance between indicator and fly. If it is fast, you may need more distance.

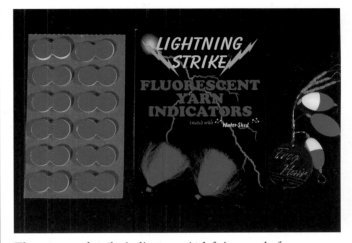

Three types of strike indicators. At left is a card of press-on strike indicators, tiny discs of foam with adhesive backing that can be pinched onto your leader. They are quick and simple to apply and also inexpensive (in the short run), but they cannot be reused. In the center are yarn swatches with braided nylon loops than can be attached to your leader with a simple knot. At the right is a group of bobber-type indicators, foam floats with two halves held together by an elastic band. To attach, you twist the halves apart, slip in your leader, and twist them shut. This type is high-floating, durable, and quite visible, but relatively expensive.

Fishing with Streamers

Streamer fishing is a stark contrast to the subtleties of nymph and dry-fly fishing. Streamers imitate minnows, which dictates a difference in how the flies are cast and retrieved and also how the trout respond to them. You may not always get as much action with streamers as with nymphs and dry flies, but you have the chance of catching some big fish and having a lot of fun in the process.

In general, streamer fishing for trout is most effective in the spring, when the water is high and murky and there is little insect activity. At such times, the trout are hungry, less discriminating, and less distracted by hatches.

A streamer box must be roomy enough to hold these long flies.

Tackle for Streamers. One glance at a collection of streamers, and it's obvious that these flies are heavier and more wind resistant than most nymphs and dry flies, so they generally require a heavier outfit. Although trout streamers in sizes 8 and smaller can be handled on light outfits, a 6-weight outfit is better for larger streamers, and an 8-weight for bigger water and weighted streamers like the popular Clouser Minnow.

A minnow is a rich meal, and big trout tend to become carnivores simply because of the difference in calories between a 3-inch minnow and a tiny insect. In fact, guides on big-trout waters often specialize in streamer fishing for trophy fish. If you are like most an-glers on most trout streams, however, you won't fish streamers all day but will try them in certain situations, such as early or late in the season in deep runs that hold big fish. Therefore, you'll usually be using an outfit lighter than ideal for streamer fishing, which means choosing streamers in the smaller sizes.

Also, when you're fishing a nymph or dry fly and switch to a streamer, you'll have to change to a heavier leader or at least tie on a new tippet—3X for smaller streamers or 2X for larger ones.

Streamer Tactics. The big difference between fishing a streamer and fishing a nymph or dry fly is that you impart a swimming action to the streamer because you want it to imitate the behavior of a fish rather than that of an insect. Unlike insects, which are at the mercy of the current, minnows can go where they want and can swim like crazy to escape predators. Whereas a trout sips helpless insects casually, it will chase and hit a streamer aggressively because the fish knows this prey can get away.

When retrieving a streamer, strip it in with your line hand a few inches at a time in little jerks, pinching the line between the thumb and forefinger of your rod hand to maintain control. It's a good idea to practice this retrieve technique in clear water on a short line so you can watch the streamer to see the action you're imparting. Experiment with the length of line you bring in on each twitch. Ideally, find some minnows to observe and see if you can mimic the way they swim in their flight from danger.

Streamer Patterns. Streamer patterns are more impressionistic than imitative, simply because fly tiers cannot imitate baitfish with hair and feathers as closely as they can imitate insects. (Innovators like Bob Popovics have used silicone and other synthetic materials to create remarkably lifelike imitations of saltwater baitfish, but that's a subject for another book.) Therefore, most anglers simply try patterns known to work on their home waters, often carrying the same pattern in a few sizes and colors rather than trying to imitate local baitfish.

The Muddler Minnow, which roughly imitates the stubby, bottom-dwelling sculpin, has proven effective everywhere. Bucktail patterns like the Black-Nose Dace and Mickey Finn imitate a more slender class of baitfish known as shiners or daces, whereas Zonkers and Matukas may approximate darters or suckers. And keep in mind that trout may mistake any large, buggy streamer (including a Woolly Bugger) fished on the bottom for crayfish, which all fish eat eagerly. As with Woolly Buggers, a general rule for streamers is to use drab or light colors and smaller sizes in clear water and vibrant or dark colors in murky water.

Covering the Water with Underwater Flies

Here is a general plan of attack for fishing any trout stream with nymphs, streamers, or wet flies. If you're new to the stream, walk the banks until you find a riffle, run, or pool you want to fish. But whatever the nature of the water, consider one limited area at a time.

When using underwater flies, you're usually prospecting for unseen fish rather than targeting individuals, but this doesn't mean spraying casts around at random. Instead, scan the water, project where fish will be, and then plot a sequence of casting positions that will let you cover these spots without spooking the fish you haven't cast to yet. In other words, cast to the nearest spots first and gradually lengthen your casts to cover the farther ones. If you do the opposite, casting to the far spots first and coming back to the near ones, you'll be fishing to water vacated by trout that you have cast or waded over.

The classic pattern for fishing underwater flies is to cast across or slightly upstream and let the fly swing downstream. Pay special attention when the fly reaches the downstream end of its drift and begins to rise, lifted by the straightened line. Fish often hit just as the fly rises off the bottom. When fishing streamers or Woolly Buggers, retrieve the fly in twitches for several feet before beginning a new cast.

After you've covered all the spots you can reach—near to far—from one casting position, take a few slow, cautious steps downstream, taking care not to kick rocks or make waves. Once you're in the new position, repeat the near-to-far casting sequence until you've covered all the water you can reach, and then move on.

If you choose to work upstream, remember the trade-off: You'll be coming at fish from their blind sides, so you can approach closer without being seen, but you'll be wading against the current, which takes more effort and can be noisy. The key is to wade slowly, lifting and placing one foot at a time.

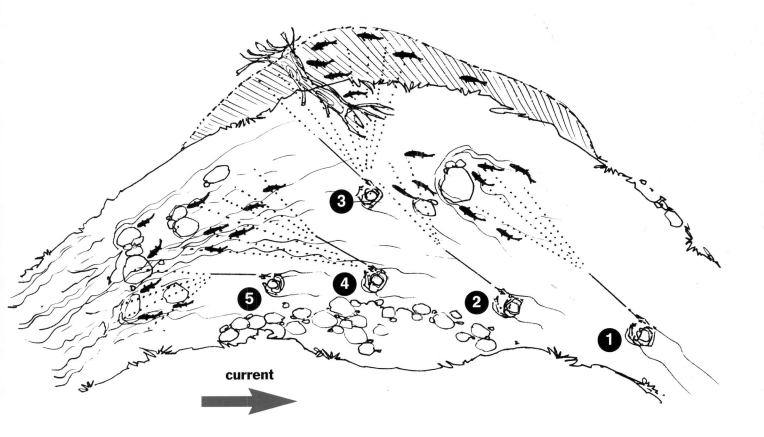

current

Casting Sequence for Underwater Flies

When sizing up a productive-looking stretch of water, identify your targets and then make a plan for covering them that won't spook the fish you haven't cast to yet. In this scenario, the angler begins at the tail of the pool, casting all around a large boulder that seems likely to hold fish. He then moves gradually upstream, stopping at each station and casting first to the downstream fish and then to those farther upstream.

FISHING WITH DRY FLIES

Dry-fly fishing for trout is a candidate for the most fun you can have fishing. Singling out a rising fish, tying on a fly you think will fool it, then making a cast and drift that present the fly convincingly enough for the trout to strike—all this is gratifying beyond words and also just sheer fun.

The visuals are what make dry-fly fishing so captivating. Most fishing involves casting to unseen quarry, wondering what's going on down there, whereas with a dry fly, it's all right there in front of you. The ultimate is finding a rising fish and casting specifically to it, but even when prospecting for unseen fish, you track the drift of the fly and watch it disappear when a trout strikes.

In ways, dry-fly fishing is more demanding than other types of fly fishing. Sometimes when the fish are feeding on a prolific hatch of insects, they'll ignore any imitation that's off by even the smallest detail. One of the most maddening experiences in all fishing is to be standing in the middle of a pool full of rising trout but not be able to get a single one to look at your fly. And in any situation, even a perfect imitation will be ignored if the line slaps down heavily, the leader lands in a pile, or the fly drifts unnaturally past the fish. In sum, the fly

has to look edible and behave naturally. Finally, dry-fly fishing to specific fish demands some accuracy in casting. You have to be able to put the fly approximately where you want it.

But trust me on this: All the effort you put into learning dry-fly fishing will be more than repaid in satisfaction and pleasure. There's just nothing like it.

First, let's define *hatch*. Most generally, it refers to the phase of an aquatic insect's life cycle during which the insect emerges from its underwater form as a nymph or pupa, transforms into a flying adult, mates, and dies. The entire process takes about two days, the sole purpose being reproduction.

Within any one hatch, then, there are several subphases, and fly patterns have been designed to imitate each one. Emerger patterns imitate a nymph or pupa that has risen to the surface and is shedding its case. Dun patterns, the largest category of dry flies, imitate a newly hatched mayfly adult that has not yet flown from the stream surface. Spinner patterns imitate the spent adult that has mated and fallen back onto the water to die.

Particular hatches may last for days or weeks, and the phases overlap. Throughout the duration, some in-

A dry-fly box must have rows or compartments with enough headroom so that the flies won't be squashed when the box is closed.

An angler studies his fly box to find a match for the evening hatch.

sects will be emerging; others will be floating on the surface, drying their newly formed wings; and still others will be falling back to the surface. In each case, the floating insects make a feast for the trout.

The hatches of virtually every trout stream in America are well documented. Their average starting and ending dates have been recorded over many years and are available in guidebooks, on regional and local websites, and at local fly shops. Some hatches are famous. The green drake hatch on Penns Creek in central Pennsylvania creates a carnival of fly fishers in early June. The blue-winged olive hatch on Montana's Yellowstone River attracts anglers from all over the country. Spend some time researching the hatches on your home water, and buy some patterns at your local shop that imitate these insects.

It's also wise to buy patterns in two or three sizes. When trout are feeding selectively, size is usually the most crucial variable, more important than color and many details of construction. Fish that are refusing a size 12 dry fly will often take a size 14 or 16 of the same pattern.

Fishing with Searching Patterns

Like all successful predators, trout are opportunists that in most situations will eat anything that looks edible, and a handful of dry flies have met this basic requirement of good searching patterns over many years. Anytime in the season after hatches begin—in most streams, early April—you can try prospecting with dry flies,

even when no fish are rising. Royal Wulffs and Elk Hair Caddis are good choices for riffles because they float high and are light colored, making them easy to track with the eye in broken water. The Adams remains one of the most productive patterns ever, simply because it looks like a lot of insects that trout eat, but its drab tones make it hard to follow in low light or choppy water. In situations where visibility is an issue, the Parachute Adams, with its white or even pink wingpost, is a better choice than the traditional pattern. In fact, many experts like the Parachute Adams in any situation, believing it sits more realistically on the water than the traditional Catskill pattern.

Casting a Dry Fly

Casting a dry fly is fly casting in its purest form. It requires more precision and attention to detail than casting underwater flies, because the manner in which a dry fly lands is often important and you're frequently casting to a particular fish. When casting a Woolly Bugger or nymph, you can get away with a cast to a general area or one with a sloppy touchdown; as long as the fly winds up drifting past a fish, you're okay. But a dry fly that lands noisily or in the wrong place, such as on top of the trout's head, is doomed.

Nevertheless, casting a dry fly is more fun and, in some ways, easier and more instructive than casting underwater flies. One advantage is that you can more clearly observe the final phase of the cast, when the leader unrolls and the fly floats down to the surface.

Watching this can help you diagnose casting problems. Also, because most trout flies are small and nearly weightless, they do not yank the leader around in the air and thus let you make a more fluid stroke. After casting weighted nymphs or streamers all morning, switching to dry flies is a pleasant relief. But part of the appeal is surely aesthetic: Casting a dry fly just feels smoother and looks better.

Choose a Target. Whenever you cast a dry fly, choose a target; don't just cast randomly into the stream. This rule is obvious when you spot a lone rising fish, but it's also true when there's a pod of rising fish or nary a dimple on the pool.

If you're in the middle of a hatch and fish are rising everywhere, watch a moment, pick out a fish, and cast to it. Despite the impression that fish are everywhere, they're not. They are in particular holding positions, each fish with its own little territory and current lane. If you cast generally, without looking over the situation, you may put your fly right on a trout's head or set up a drift over empty water. By choosing a target, you're assured of getting a good shot at a fish, and you may even get lucky. If this trout ignores your fly, another may be downstream in the same lane.

Searching with dry flies when no fish are rising can be productive too. But even then, pick out a specific

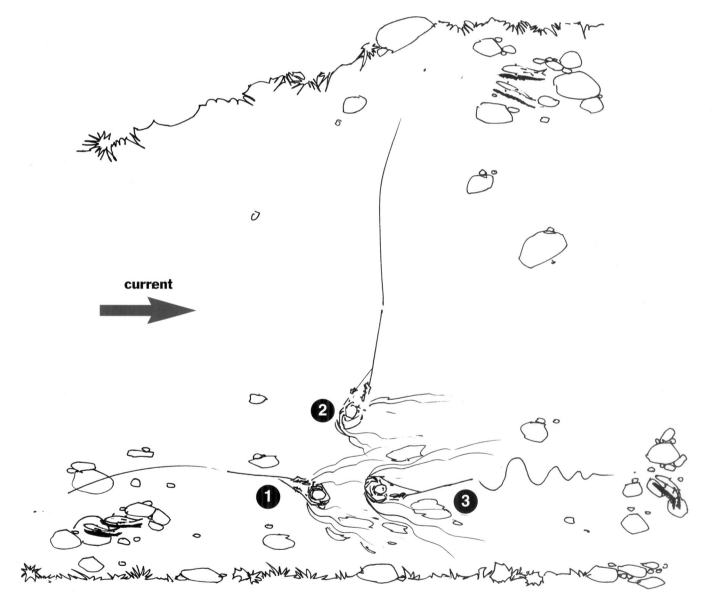

current

(1) When targeting upstream fish with a dry fly, aim a few feet upstream of the fish and a bit to one side. Don't cast right over it, as the leader or line may spook it. (2) When casting across a stream, again aim for a spot a few feet above the fish, but watch your distance: Try to place the fly so that it drifts in front of the trout's nose rather than directly over it. (3) When casting to downstream fish, use a slack-line or wiggle cast that places the fly several feet upstream of the fish, and then let the current carry it by it.

place and imagine a fish there. Your target may be the pocket behind a rock or where the current sweeps beneath an undercut bank. Or it may be a little broader, a current lane at the head of a pool where you've seen fish rising before.

Where the Fly Should Land. Once you've found a target, try to put the fly a foot or two upstream of the trout or holding place, so the fish can easily see the fly and does not have to go too far to get it. Rarely will a trout turn to strike a fly that lands behind it, and rarely will the fish swim more than a few feet from its holding spot to take the fly. But you don't want the fly to land right on top of the fish's head, a sure way to spook it.

Beyond these general rules, where you want the fly to land in relation to the fish depends on whether you're casting up-, across-, or downstream. If you're casting directly upstream, aim your cast a little to one side of the trout so you don't lay the line on top of it, a blunder called lining the fish. One of the advantages to casting upstream is that you can overshoot your fish by quite a bit and the fly will still eventually drift past its nose.

When casting across-stream to a target, you again must place the fly upstream of the fish or holding spot, but the length of the cast must be a bit more precise. If you cast too far, the current will bring the fly behind or your line directly over the trout, whereas if you cast too short, the fly may drift beyond the fish's striking range. Remember this general rule: The fly should drift a foot or so in front of the fish's nose.

Presenting a fly to a downstream fish requires line control more than casting accuracy, but one rule still applies: You must put your fly upstream of the trout and let it drift by the fish's nose. The advantage of casting to a trout that is downstream from you is that because it's facing upstream, the fly drifts by the fish before the leader and line.

Introducing Slack. The problem with casting downstream is that once the fly lands, it begins to drag almost instantly because it's already at the end of its tether, prevented from continuing downstream by the straightened line. The solution is to introduce some slack, either with the slack-line cast or, if you need less slack, with a simple technique called a wiggle cast. To do this, make a normal forward cast, but on the forward stroke, while the line is still in the air, wiggle the rod tip from side to side. This motion will create waves in the line as it falls, so it lands on the water in curves rather than in a straight line. The fly thus has some time to drift before it is pulled up short by the straightened line.

When to Start the Next Cast. If you make a bad cast to a fish—if the fly lands too short or long or in an ugly pile of leader—resist the natural impulse to rip it off the water immediately and cast again. All that will accomplish is spooking the fish. On any cast, let the fly drift far past the trout before picking up your line to make the next cast.

Another trick when casting to a rising fish is to time your cast to its next anticipated rise. Trout tend to rise in a rhythm. The timing may be determined by how hungry the fish is or how many insects are on the water, and it may even vary from the beginning of the hatch, when the trout is eager and famished, to the end, when it is gorged. But if you can pick up this timing, you have a better chance of presenting your fly just when the fish is ready.

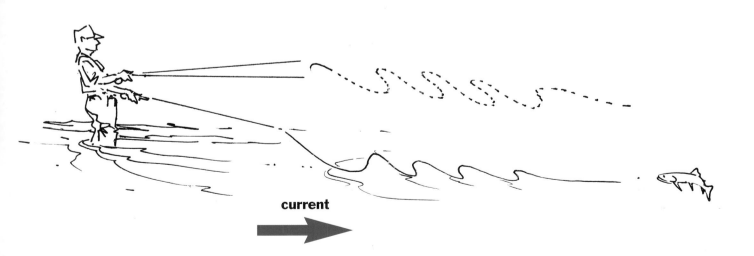

current

To do a wiggle cast, simply wave your rod back and forth after you stop it on the forward stroke, as the fly is dropping. This motion will make the line land on the water in waves, allowing your fly a brief, drag-free drift to downstream fish.

DRAG-FREE DRIFT

Drag is the motion of a fly being pulled through the water faster than, or against, the current—in other words, unnaturally. Drag happens most commonly when a fly is cast across-stream and the current catches the fly line, pulling the line downstream in a belly and dragging the fly along behind it. This situation is caused in part by the fact that fly line is thick and buoyant and more easily caught by the current than the leader. Drag also occurs when the line straightens downstream at the end of a drift and the fly suddenly stops dead or begins moving upstream. Insects don't behave like this, and trout know it.

You encounter the least problems with drag when casting upstream, simply because the line is aligned with the current so there's not a cross-stream length of it to be caught and dragged downstream. Instead, it will drift toward you at something like the rate of the fly, and as long as you strip in the excess line with your line hand, the fly will drift naturally.

Drag is most obvious when fishing a dry fly, because a wake forms behind the fly that is visible to both fish and fisher. But drag affects underwater flies as well and is particularly problematic in nymph fishing, when the trout are watching these small insects floating drag-free downstream all day. A number of techniques are used to fight drag.

current

When you cast across-stream, the current pulls the line downstream in a belly, which in turn drags the fly along behind it, creating an unnaturally fast drift.

current

Drag is also created when a fly reaches the end of its tether, directly downstream from you; it stops dead in the current, a sure giveaway that it's a counterfeit.

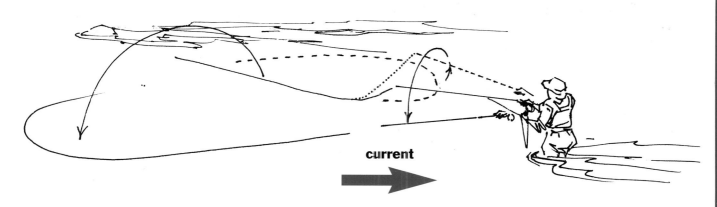

To mend line, lift your rod and move it in a rolling motion upstream. This will reposition the portion of the line lying on the water so it does not form a belly and drag your fly downstream.

Plan Your Cast

The first strategy to avoid drag is simply scanning the water beforehand and visualizing the fly's drift. You want to avoid casting across water that has differing current speeds—across a fast channel into a slow eddy or across a flat into a channel. If you cast across fast water into slow, the fast water will catch your line and drag it downstream, the fly behind it. If you cast across slow water into fast, the fly will race downstream and get pulled up short by the lagging line. If possible, always move to a position where your cast will travel across water of uniform current.

If you're fishing in a slow or moderate current, an upstream or three-quarter upstream cast will give you a reasonably long drag-free drift if you simply point your rod tip at the fly and follow it as it drifts. As the fly swings downstream, lowering your rod tip and extending your arm will lengthen the drag-free drift by a few feet.

Slack-Line Casts

In complex currents or in situations where your target is in slow water and a fast lane of current intervenes between you and it, you can adjust your forward cast to create slack in the line while it's still in the air so that it lands on the surface in curves.

Mending Line

Mending line is a technique of eliminating drag after you have cast by lifting line off the water and repositioning it upstream so it cannot pull the fly downstream. After your cast settles on the water, lift your rod tip and move it in a rolling motion upstream, as if you were lifting the line over a low fence just upstream of where you are. At the moment you begin this motion, release the line with your line hand, or else the rolling motion of your rod will jerk the fly upstream as well. In some cases, you may have to mend line several times during one drift to keep the line upstream of the fly.

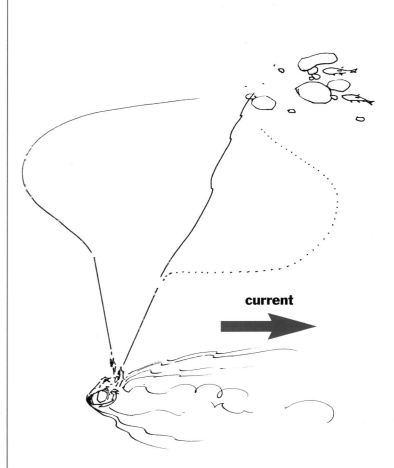

The dotted line to the right shows the belly that would form in the line if it were allowed to be pulled downstream by the current. The solid line to the left shows the position of the line after an upstream mend.

High Sticking

High sticking, a technique specific to nymph fishing, is a way of reducing drag by lifting your rod tip high during the drift in order to keep as much line as possible off the water so the current can't catch it. High sticking works only at short range and with long leaders, because you can lift just so much line off the water by lifting the rod. The technique also has the disadvantage of putting the rod in a bad position for setting the hook: It's already in the hook-set position and can't be brought back much farther. In situations where you can wade close to the riffle or channel you want to fish, however, high sticking can be deadly. You simply flip the fly into the head of the stretch; hold your rod high enough to keep all but the leader out of the water, if you can; and let the nymph drift down through, following it with your rod tip.

High sticking is a technique for reducing drag when fishing nymphs at short range. Hold the rod high enough that the fly line is off the water and only the leader is underwater. Follow the nymph downstream with your rod.

Trout spit out flies quickly—it doesn't take them long to realize their mistake—so you must respond the moment you detect a hit by snapping your rod tip up and back. This motion need not be violent, but it must be quick, not slow. It must also be done with a taut line, rather than a slack one, or the effect of your rod motion will be to straighten the line, not set the hook. This is another reason to strip in unwanted slack as you fish, so you're ready to set the hook when a fish takes.

Small flies don't require a muscular hook set, because the small-diameter point penetrates very easily, like a thin wire nail into a piece of soft pine. Sometimes all you have to do is lift the rod quickly. Even with a very small fly, however, you still need a taut line and a quick response to hook the fish before it ejects the fly. In fact, if you have the slack out of your line, trout will often hook themselves when they strike aggressively or faster than you can react. With larger flies, sizes 8 and up, and bigger fish, you may need a more forceful snap to drive the hook in.

Once you set the hook and feel the fish on—an electrifying sensation with a fly rod—keep that rod tip high for the duration of the fight. You can bring in average-size trout (8 to 15 inches or so) the same way you retrieve a fly, by stripping in line with your line hand and pinching it with the fingers of your rod hand to keep the regained line from being pulled back out. Don't horse the fish in, but do pull it in as soon as it's willing

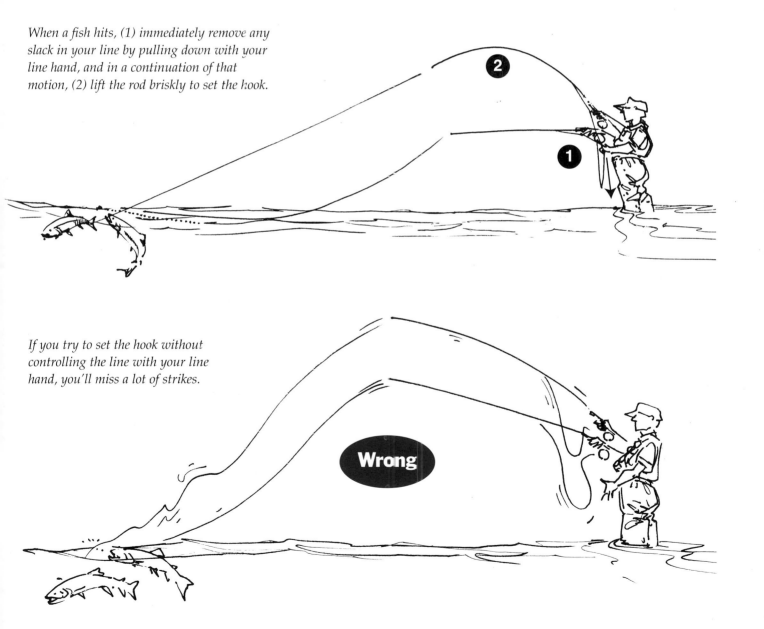

When a fish hits, (1) immediately remove any slack in your line by pulling down with your line hand, and in a continuation of that motion, (2) lift the rod briskly to set the hook.

If you try to set the hook without controlling the line with your line hand, you'll miss a lot of strikes.

so you can release it unharmed. A trout can wear itself out quickly.

Larger fish may have to be played off the reel. If you hook a heavy fish and it makes a run, let it take out any coils of line in your line hand, keeping tension on the line with your rod-hand fingers, and then grab the reel handle with your line hand. At this point, let your reel's drag do the work. If it's been preset to the right point, it will give out line before the fish pulls hard enough to snap your tippet. The right setting depends on the size of the fish and the test strength of your tippet. If you hook a 3-pound trout on a 7X tippet, you'll be in a panic to loosen that drag knob. In some cases, you may have to adjust the drag during a fight, loosening it to absorb the early lunges of a big fish, tightening it as the fish tires.

Landing a fish with a fly rod is awkward because the rod is so long. Your goal is to guide the fish to your hand, but in order to reach it, you have to hold the rod vertical but tilted away and somewhat behind you. Avoid retrieving the line so far that you pull the leader-line knot through your tip-top rod guide, as playing a thrashing fish with nothing but a length of leader extending from your rod tip is asking for a break-off. But if your leader is longer than your rod, the fish is thus on an even longer tether. A net helps in landing fish because it extends your reach by a foot or so. If you're landing a fish by hand, you'll have to pull it in a little closer. In either case, try to dislodge the hook without lifting the fish completely out of the water. If you're using a barbless hook—as you should—you can usually free it with a short tug.

Maintain tension on a hooked fish by pulling down with your line hand to remove slack and keeping the rod tip high to absorb his runs.

When landing a fish, hold your rod tip high.

94

6

Fly-Fishing for Bass and Pike

From its origins as a method for trout, fly fishing has expanded to warm-water species such as bass, pike, and carp. When switching to these species, the first adaptation the trout fisher must make is to heavier equipment; although the basic casting technique is the same as for trout, the flies are heavier and more wind resistant, and the fish are generally bigger.

If you plan to do a lot of fishing for bass and pike or venture into salt water, an 8-weight outfit is a good investment. An 8-weight is heavy enough for just about any freshwater gamefish and will also serve as a coastal and light surf-fishing outfit. If you already own a 6- or 7-weight outfit for heavy trout fishing, you can use it for bass, but you'll find it somewhat light for casting large bugs or weighted flies and certainly too light for casting big pike streamers or playing 10-pound fish.

Reel

The larger the fish, the more important the reel's drag. As you move from trout to big bass and especially to pike, you'll want a reel with a disk drag to handle the runs of big fish. Also buy at least one extra spool, as bass and pike fishing often requires switching from floating to sinking lines or specialty tapers.

Line

In most situations, a floating line is best for bass and pike, and a weight-forward taper is a good all-around choice. Match the weight of the line to the outfit. Thus for an 8-weight rod, start with a WF-8-F line. Because the leader sinks, a sinking fly can get down to depths of 4 or 5 feet, even on a floating line. To get down a little deeper, you can lengthen your leader, add split shot, or switch to a heavier fly.

For fishing at depths of more than 4 feet or so, you may need a sinking-tip line. The middle range, III and IV, are most useful; they'll get your fly down quickly but are easier to cast than the faster-sinking versions, V

and VI. Sinking-tip lines are particularly useful when fishing a stretch of river that's not very deep but has a current that keeps a fly from getting down.

For fishing water 6 to 30 feet deep or for trolling, you'll need a full-sinking line. Before you invest in such line, though, consider the fact that fly fishing is not the most efficient or enjoyable method for deep water. Before you can cast a deeply sunk line, you must haul most of it in rather than just picking it up off the surface, as you can with a floating line. Thus casting a sinking line is a chore.

If you'll be casting large poppers and bugs regularly, consider a bass bug taper, a specialty line with a shorter, thicker front section than a normal weight-forward line.

Backing

Although hooked bass or pike rarely make long runs like some saltwater gamefish—notably bonefish and false albacore, which can take all the fly line off your reel in seconds—a big bass or pike will sometimes dive for the bottom of a lake or head downstream in a river, and you don't want to find out the hard way that you don't have enough backing. An 8-weight reel has room for at least 150 yards of Dacron backing, and putting on this amount not only gives you insurance against long runs, but also provides the added benefit of letting you retrieve more line with each crank of the reel handle, since the wound backing effectively increases the diameter of the arbor.

When fishing for bass and pike, you will often be on water that is bigger and windier than a trout stream, and you'll need to make longer casts with wind-resistant flies and a heavy outfit. The double haul is essential in such situations. It is a technique for getting more distance and power from a forward cast by making quick, precisely timed tugs, or hauls, on the line with your line hand during the backcast and forward stroke. These tugs increase the casting distance because they increase the speed of the line shooting out. This may seem counterintuitive, as you're tugging the line in a direction opposite to which it is being cast. But the double haul works because the tugs put a sudden, additional load on the rod tip, causing it to snap straight more rapidly and accelerate the line more quickly than it would in a normal cast.

1. START: Hands together.

2. Rod lifts, beginning the backcast; hands still together.

3. Near the speed-up-stop, **haul** . . .

4. speed-up-**stop** and . . .

7. hands come back . . .

8. together.

5. line straightens . . .

6. behind you . . .

9. START THE FORECAST: Hands together.

10. Rod leads the cast . . .

99

11. approaching speed-up-stop, **haul** . . .

12. speed-up-**stop** and . . .

15. together.

16. Cast is complete as line travels out to target.

13. hands come . . .

14. back . . .

In *Modern Fly-Casting Methods*, Lefty Kreh observes that the most common mistake in double hauling is making hauls that are too long, that is, pulling back too much line with the line hand on each haul. A short, fast tug, no more than 18 inches, accomplishes the goal (greater line speed) much more efficiently than a long, slow one. A long haul also creates slack that can slap and tangle with your rod.

Timing is key. As you recall, the crucial element in Lefty's casting method is the speed-up-and-stop at the end of each stroke. He recommends you begin each haul just as you accelerate your rod for the speed-up-and-stop and end it when you stop the rod. This in itself will limit the length of your haul, as the speed-up-and-stop is a crisp motion at the very end of the stroke. Ideally, the length of the haul—the distance you pull the line—should match the distance your rod hand moves during the speed-up-and-stop.

1. Hands . . .

2. together . . .

5. hands . . .

6. come . . .

9. hands . . .

10. together . . .

13. hands . . .

14. come . . .

3. back . . .

4. haul . . .

7. back . . .

8. together . . .

11. forward . . .

12. haul . . .

15. back . . .

16. together.

103

Smallmouth bass are a blast on a fly rod, especially in rivers, where they can be caught in shallow water and behave like bigger, rougher cousins of trout. Pugnacious and acrobatic, they're often called the hardest-fighting fish in fresh water.

Bass Leaders

You can use knotless tapered leaders for bass fishing, but they must be heavier than those for trout. A 3X leader is about as light as you'll ever need for bass, with the possible exception of when dry-fly fishing for smallmouths in clear water, in which case you might go down to a 4X. For large bass in weedy water, a 0X leader or heavier may be necessary. For streamers or other underwater flies, 7 or 8 feet of 6- or 8-pound-test monofilament will suffice as a leader, because you're not concerned about how the leader turns over and sets the fly down on the water.

Smallmouth Habitat

Smallmouth bass seek water with a rocky bottom, as opposed to the weedy habitat of largemouth bass, and also require slightly colder water than largemouths. Smallmouth rivers are typically rocky and riffled, and in a lake that holds both species of bass, you'll generally find the smallmouths around rocky shorelines, ledges, and shoals and the largemouths around lily pads and submerged weed beds. Both species tend to hang around structure in the water, such as downed logs and boat docks.

Like all fish in moving water, smallmouth bass in rivers seek spots where they can lie in wait for prey, fac-ing upstream, with some relief from the current. One of the most obvious places to try is the slack water behind rocks, and you'll find plenty of rocks in a smallmouth river. Smallmouths will also hold in riffles, especially those that are at least a foot deep and have eddies or rocks as ambush spots. They may be anywhere in a deep pool, but especially around the heads and tails or behind submerged rocks.

Where you find one smallmouth, you'll usually find more, because they congregate in areas where food is plentiful. So if you catch one, keep working that area with the same fly.

Streamer Fishing for Smallmouths

Much of trout-fishing technique can be applied to smallmouth bass fishing, and at times you can even catch bass on trout flies. But the bulk of a smallmouth's diet is not small aquatic insects, but bigger and more diversified food forms, including minnows, crayfish, and hellgrammites. Also, whereas in trout fishing it is often crucial to match the size of the insect on which the trout are feeding and a tiny fly frequently will catch a huge fish, a general rule in bass fishing is that bigger flies catch bigger fish. Streamers are the most popular type of flies for smallmouths because they imitate baitfish, a main food source of bass everywhere.

Streamer Patterns

The Clouser Minnow, one of the most successful streamer patterns in the world, was developed specifically for smallmouth bass by legendary Susquehanna River guide Bob Clouser. Its distinguishing feature is

Although all smallmouth bass have a bronze hue, their markings vary widely. Many have distinctly barred flanks, like this beauty from an Ontario river.

the dumbbell weight just behind the hook eye, which simulates minnow eyes and, more important, makes the fly sink quickly and gives it a jigging action. A third feature of this weight, however, is that it makes a Clouser Minnow unwieldy to cast with a light rod. So although a 5-weight trout rod can easily handle an average-size river smallmouth, it lacks the backbone to cast a Clouser, especially into the wind. Bob Clouser and Lefty Kreh, the two most famous smallmouth fly fishermen in the world, prefer an 8-weight outfit for smallmouth bass, which should tell you something. Clousers are tied in a variety of colors. Chartreuse is probably the most popular, but you should have two or three other colors on hand, as bass often prefer a different color because of water clarity or the type of minnows they're feeding on.

The Muddler Minnow, which is used for trout in smaller sizes (8, 10, and 12), is also a great bass pattern in larger sizes, 2, 4, and 6. This streamer imitates a sculpin, a bottom-dwelling baitfish, and should be bumped along the bottom. Therefore, choose the weighted variety when ordering from a catalog or selecting flies in a store. You can also add a split shot to your leader about a foot above the fly to get the streamer down to the fish.

Legendary smallmouth guide Bob Clouser casts to classic smallmouth habitat, a rock-bottomed pool above a ledge in the Susquehanna River.

Clouser Deep Minnow

Baby Smallmouth Clouser

Clouser Darter Perch

Streamer Tactics

You fish a streamer in a smallmouth river much as you would for trout in a stream, by casting it up-, across-, or downstream and giving it a lifelike swimming motion when stripping in line.

As in trout fishing, aim your cast beyond likely holding places, so your fly doesn't land on the bass's head but your retrieve brings it by the fish's window of vision. When retrieving, strip in about a foot of line at a time with your line hand, keeping the rod tip low and pointed at the fly. Don't give the fly action by jigging your rod tip back and forth or up and down, as this motion creates slack in the line, a hindrance to setting the hook. Bass hit streamers suddenly and hard, and though a fish sometimes hooks itself in the process, a taut line will help prevent it from spitting out the fly.

In fact, always keep your line hand on your line. When casting upstream in a fast current, you must be ready to strip in slack line the instant the fly lands, and you'll have to keep stripping as the streamer drifts toward you to prevent slack from accumulating. Bass often hit a streamer right after it lands, and if you've let the current pull a belly in your line, you won't be able set the hook on quick strikes. As the streamer swings across- and downstream, the current will take the slack out of the line, and occasional twitches are all you need to make the fly behave like a minnow. When the streamer reaches the end of its tether directly downstream, bring it back toward you in lifelike twitches. Don't bring it back all the way, though; bass seldom hit a fly that's been retrieved all the way up to you or the boat, and anyway, it's easier to start the next cast if you already have some line out.

This chunky smallmouth, fooled by a black popper, lacks the distinct markings of the one on page 104.

Bob Clouser drifts the Susquehanna in his jon boat, casting a Clouser Minnow along the shoreline of an island. Like trout, smallmouths tend to hang behind rocks or obstructions that provide cover and relief from the current.

A traditional bass popper with cork body

A bass popper with rubber legs

To refine your retrieve technique, it's instructive to observe real minnows. When you spot some, often in schools in shallow water, watch their darting movements when spooked and try to mimic it with your retrieve. Then dunk your streamer in the water at close range, where you can see it, and experiment with the length and rhythm of your stripping movement.

A tip on streamer and popper retrieves is to hold the rod in front of you and toward your line hand side (the left, for right-handed casters) rather than on your rod-hand side while stripping in the fly. This lets you bring your line hand back straight as you strip in line, whereas if you hold the rod as usual, on the rod-hand side (the right, for right-handed casters), you have to strip in the line across your body, at a right angle to the stripping guide, which limits the length and force of your strips.

When fishing in slow, deep river pools or a lake, you have let the streamer sink before beginning your retrieve. Even in this situation, though, remember to keep the slack out of your line.

Woolly Buggers are deadly on bass, which probably mistake them for hellgrammites, the larval stage of the dobsonfly. These large, nasty aquatic insects, which can pinch you painfully, crawl around rocks on the river bottom, and bass eat them whenever they can get at them. The same Woolly Bugger patterns you use for trout will work for bass, but use larger sizes, 4 and 6, and weight them.

Cast directly or three-quarters upstream and let the fly bump along the bottom. Pay attention as your line straightens downstream, though, as bass often hit a Woolly Bugger just as it rises at the end of its drift. When fishing Woolly Buggers in a lake, let the fly sink to the bottom of a rocky drop-off or shoal and bring it back in short twitches.

Poppers

Poppers are surface lures with bodies of cork, Styrofoam, or deer hair and tails and legs of feathers or plastic. The bass most likely take them for frogs, but they may also imitate wounded minnows or even large insects struggling on the surface. The front of a popper is shaped to make a *pop* on the surface when retrieved in sharp tugs. It takes a little practice with your line hand to get the feel for this technique—the tugs must be short and quick, unlike the longer and smoother tugs used to retrieve a streamer. Bass in a river respond primarily to the noise and movement of surface lures, so keep your popper moving and making noise. Poppers are especially effective in flat water or smooth runs in the morning and evening, when the water is cool and the bass are close to the surface. They are less effective on choppy water, such as riffles or wave-ruffled pools, because they are less visible and audible to the fish.

Bass can be hard to hook on poppers. Often you'll see a big splash only to find the bass has missed the fly entirely. Or, like most of us, you'll strike too soon and yank the popper out of the fish's mouth. It is actually better to wait a beat after the strike, giving the bass a chance to inhale the popper. Wait till you feel the fish on the line before setting the hook.

107

Largemouth bass have been the most popular gamefish in America for generations, even before the professional bass tournament transformed bass fishing into a multi-billion-dollar industry. Since then, spinning and bait-casting tackle and technique have been developed for every conceivable situation and type of largemouth bass water. In truth, largemouth habitat is not ideal for fly fishing, because the fish favor weedy areas in lakes, water that is usually deeper and more difficult to fish with flies than with conventional lures like plugs, jigs, and plastic worms, which can be made virtually weedless and are easily worked at precise depths. In short, if your focus is largemouth bass, spinning and bait-casting tackle is the best way to go. Still, largemouths can be had on the fly rod, and they are especially fun on the surface. You can use the same outfit, including the line and leaders, as for smallmouth bass.

Largemouth Habitat

Largemouths can be found in slow rivers, but they prefer mud bottoms and aquatic weeds and are therefore principally stillwater fish. They are found all over the continent, from the farm ponds of the Midwest to the forested lakes of southern Ontario and the giant reservoirs of the South and West.

Wherever they live, largemouths seek underwater structure. You'll find them among aquatic weed beds; under boat docks, logs, and overhanging trees; and around shoals or points of land that extend into the lake. They also seek shade, especially in the heat of summer.

Except for the smallest farm ponds and shallowest lakes, largemouth fishing involves a boat, and the key to success in lakes is moving from one likely structure to the next. Bass don't hang in schools, per se. If an underwater structure is small, such as a single log in the water, you may find one bass under it. If the structure is large—a vast weed bed, a bay of stumps, a big willow tree with branches drooping into the water—you may find many bass around it. The point is, to catch bass consistently in a lake, you need to keep moving. If you catch one near a small structure, such as a downed log or a boat dock, there's not likely to be another bass in exactly the same spot. If the area is slightly larger, you may make a few more casts, but don't linger. Likewise, when fishing a shoreline with several overhanging trees, don't spend too much time at each one; hit them all.

Fishing with Poppers and Bass Bugs

Casting a popper or bass bug to the edges and holes in weed beds is a thoroughly enjoyable way to catch largemouths in a lake. Largemouth bass hang around weeds, waiting for frogs and minnows, and they'll often smash a popper or bug cast to the right spot.

Bass bugs and poppers are large and wind resistant, and the bass bug taper was created to cast them. Its front section is thicker and shorter than a conventional weight-forward taper, which is like putting a bigger head on a hammer handle; you generate more power when you swing it, because the head is moving faster at the end of the swing.

Bass in Lily Pads

The most effective and often the only way to fish lily pads is from a boat. The water under lily pad beds can be more than chest-deep, and largemouth lakes often have mucky bottoms, so wading around these beds is usually not an option.

Casting a bug or popper around lily pads requires accuracy. Largemouth bass station themselves right under the pads, both for protection from predators and concealment from prey, and they won't move far into open water to hit something. Ideally, your popper or bug should land within inches of the pads—sometimes

Flip Pallot releases a nice largemouth that hit a popper in Florida's St. John's River.

A small inflatable boat is handy for cruising among lily pads in backcountry lakes and ponds, casting poppers for bass.

The Bendback, with its angled hook shank, can be retrieved through even heavy weeds without hanging up.

The Dahlberg Diving Bug, created by bass fly-fishing legend Larry Dahlberg, is a proven pattern for bass.

a foot is too far away. Then again, you must avoid over-shooting your mark and putting your fly onto the pads. Lily pads and stalks are tough material, and if you hook one, you'll have to row in there to free your fly, spooking the fish in the bargain. The best strategy is to cast parallel to a line of pads and retrieve the popper or bug as close to the edge as you can.

The strategy for popper fishing is different in a lake than in a river. In the current of a river, you have to keep a popper popping so the bass recognizes it as a living morsel among the other stuff floating overhead. In a lake, a bass has more time to inspect its prey, and a popper left motionless for a few moments after it lands, then twitched, often triggers a strike. This behavior may mimic that of frogs, which sit motionless on lily pads or the surface of the water.

The real test of precision casting is placing a popper in an opening in a lily pad bed. A bass surrounded by pads feels more secure than one on the edge, and holes in pads often draw strikes. If you hook a large bass in the middle of the pads, though, it can be a struggle to get the fish out. Its first response will be to dive into the

lily pad stalks, a key reason for using stout leaders when bass-fishing in the weeds.

Streamer Fishing for Largemouths

Minnows are a main food of largemouth bass, and you can use the same streamer patterns as for smallmouths. The difference is that in most cases, you'll be fishing in a lake and not a river, so you'll be casting to underwater structure rather than working the fly in the current.

A favorite largemouth habitat in summer is an aquatic weed bed in 6 to 12 feet of water, and you may need to use a split shot or sinking line to get down to these fish. Especially in the middle of a summer day, you won't find bass in the warm upper layer of open water. One approach to fishing weed beds is to cast right among the weeds with a weedless streamer, such as the Bend Back, which, if retrieved slowly, will come through even relatively thick weeds without hanging up. Another is to cast a proven pattern like a Clouser Minnow or Dahlberg Diver parallel to the bed and retrieve it in twitches as close to the edge of the weeds as possible.

109

Pike

Fly-fishing for pike has become increasingly popular among anglers who enjoy casting big flies for big fish. Pike are fast growing. Most pike lakes hold scores of fish in the 20-inch, 2- to 3-pound range and a good number over 30 inches and up to 10 or 15 pounds. A 40-inch, 20-pound pike is a lunker almost anywhere, and in trophy pike lakes in northern Canada, the fish can reach 50 inches and 50 pounds.

Pike Tackle

An 8-weight outfit is suitable for most pike fishing, although a 9-weight is preferable for really big fish. If you're buying a rod specifically for pike, get the fastest action available. The stiffer the rod, the better it will throw large flies and handle big fish.

A reel with a strong, smooth disk drag is an absolute necessity to absorb the sudden, powerful lunges for which pike are notorious. These bursts often occur on a short line, when you've brought the fish almost all the way in and you think it's finished. Although pike don't tend to run far, as some saltwater species like bonefish do, they can put up an extended fight, slicing back and forth, giving line and taking it back. One snap of the pike's long, snakelike body can propel it back down to the depths, and if your reel doesn't give line smoothly, a big fish can snap your tippet or straighten

your hook. In any case, fishing for big pike is the acid test of knot tying.

A weight-forward floating line is the best choice, because when fly-fishing for pike, you'll be targeting fish in shallow water. In most lakes, except for those in the far north, pike migrate into deep water when the upper layer warms above 70 degrees, and they're then beyond the reach of fly fishers.

A pike leader must be heavy and tough enough to handle large fish and withstand slicing teeth. It need not be tapered, because it doesn't need to unfurl gracefully and set a fly down naturally, as a trout leader must. The simplest solution is a 9-foot length of 20-pound-test monofilament. Some companies, such as Rio, make hard monofilament leader material designed to resist the abrasion of toothy species like pike and barracuda. Braided wire gives even more protection against pike teeth, and special pike leaders are available with wire tippets attached to monofilament butt sections.

Pike Tactics

In most lakes, the best time to fly-fish for pike is in the spring, just after ice-out, when the water warms to the midfifties and the pike move into the shallows to spawn. Depending on latitude, this can occur anywhere from late April to late May. As always, local information is the key. Ask around or check guidebooks or websites for the date when pike fishing begins to pick up on a particular lake or river.

Ed Jaworowski holds a 20-pound pike caught on a streamer in Hatchet Lake, Saskatchewan.

Barry's Pike Fly, created by Barry Reynolds, is a great all-around pike and muskie streamer.

Lefty's Deceiver, perhaps the most popular saltwater pattern of all time, is also deadly on pike.

Weedy bays in northern lakes are prime pike habitat, especially in the spring, when pike move into the shallows to spawn, and in the fall, when water temperatures cool down and bring the fish out of deeper water to feed.

During the spring spawning period, look for fish in shallow, weedy bays. Places where creeks enter a lake or river are especially good. Often such water is accessible by wading, but you can also fish it from a boat. Guides and experienced pike fishers learn to spot fish in the shallows and stalk them, but pike are well camouflaged and hard to see, so your best bet is to cover a likely area with casts.

Large, flashy streamers, 3 to 8 inches long, are good bets for pike. Veteran pike guide Barry Reynolds, who, with John Berryman, literally wrote the book on fly-fishing for pike, called *Pike on the Fly*, lists the Bunny Bug—sold as Barry's Pike Fly—as his favorite all-around pike fly. It can be fished shallow or deep, depending on whether you're using a floating or sinking line, and includes a weedguard made of thick monofilament. The ever-popular Lefty's Deceiver is another excellent choice for pike, especially in deeper water. The weedless Bend Back streamer, the same as described for largemouth bass but in larger sizes, is good for retrieving through thick weeds.

Black and chartreuse are two of the most common colors for pike streamers, but red and white is also a proven combination. Streamers 6 inches long and up, especially those of rabbit fur, may require a 9-weight rod to cast effectively. Rabbit fur's drawback is that it gets very heavy when wet. Still, it's a popular material for pike flies because of its undulating action in the water and also because it's tough enough to resist shredding by pike teeth.

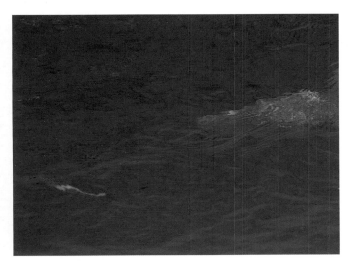

Pike sometimes have the maddening habit of following a fly right back to the rod tip without striking, like this one that's chasing an orange and yellow Lefty's Deceiver. If you are getting a lot of follows without strikes, try swishing your rod tip back and forth in a figure-eight motion at the very end of the retrieve, or simply speeding up the retrieve. Sometimes this added action—perhaps imitating a panicked baitfish—will trigger a strike. Another tactic, recommended by pike expert Barry Reynolds (Pike on the Fly) is to switch from a wire to a less visible monofilament leader.

Resources

BOOKS

The Cast, Ed Jaworowski. Stackpole Books, 1992.
One of the most thorough, detailed, and graphic examinations of casting technique ever written. With black and white photos by Lefty Kreh.

Fly Fishing Basics, Dave Hughes. Stackpole Books, 1994.
A perennial favorite because it explains so concisely the essentials of the sport. No one writes more clearly than Hughes or offers such sound advice. With line drawings by Richard Bunse.

Fly-Fishing the Flats, Barry and Cathy Beck. Stackpole Books, 1999.
A practical and beautifully illustrated guide to fly fishing salt water.

Modern Fly-Casting Methods, Lefty Kreh. Lyons Press, 2003.
A compact, crisply illustrated guide to essential casting techniques. Line drawings by Rod Walinchus.

The Orvis Fly-Fishing Guide, Tom Rosenbauer. Lyons Press, 1988.
A well-written, comprehensive guide to all aspects of the sport. With black and white photos, drawings, and tables.

Pike on the Fly, Barry Reynolds and John Berryman. Johnson Books, 1993.
The definitive work on fly-fishing for pike and musky.

Practical Fishing Knots, Mark Sosin and Lefty Kreh. Lyons Press, 1991.
Second edition of a standard reference that has been in print for more than thirty years. Clear, easy-to-follow instructions for fifty knots. With drawings by Rod Walinchus.

Presenting the Fly, Lefty Kreh. Lyons Press, 1999.
A thick book packed with tips on casting, tackle, and technique for all species of gamefish.

Reading the Water, Dave Hughes. Stackpole Books, 1988.
A compact, readable guide to evaluating different types of trout water—riffles, runs, pools, flats, lakes—and how to fish them.

Spring Creeks, Mike Lawson. Stackpole Books, 2003.
A richly photographed and illustrated hardbound guide to fishing spring creeks, focusing on those in the West, from a veteran Montana guide, tier, and fly-shop owner.

Troubleshooting the Cast, Ed Jaworowski. Stackpole Books, 1999.
An illustrated workbook on how to recognize and correct the most common casting problems, such as tailing loops and sagging backcasts. With line drawings.

GUIDES TO AQUATIC INSECTS

An Angler's Guide to Aquatic Insects and Their Imitations, Rick Hafele and Scott Roederer. Johnson Books, 1995.
A very handy book, with black and white illustrations giving keys to identification and lists of patterns that imitate each species.

Handbook of Hatches Second ed., Dave Hughes. Stackpole Books, 2005.
A comprehensive guide to hatches of all significant aquatic insects and how to fish them. With color photos of insects and fly patterns.

Instant Mayfly Identification Guide, Al Caucci and Bob Nastasi. Caucci Flyfishing Enterprises, 1984.
A small, spiral-bound field guide that fits in your pocket. With color plates and line drawings showing step-by-step identification of mayfly nymphs and adults.

VIDEO

Lefty Kreh on Fly Casting, Reel Resources, 2004.
One-hour DVD. An invaluable guide to the fundamentals of casting. Includes demonstrations of Lefty's four basic principles, as explained in chapter 3 of this book, along with how they are applied to the forward cast, roll cast, and several specialty casts.